SCHOLASTIC
ATLAS
OF THE
UNITED
STATES

SCHOLASTIC
ATLAS
OF THE
UNITED
STATES

David Rubel

An Agincourt Press Book

To Abraham Rosman and Robert Schmeling, on their seventieth
and eightieth years, respectively

Copy Editor: Ron Boudreau
Proofreader: Laura Jorstad

Art Direction and Production: Oxygen Design
Interior Design, Maps, Illustrations: Sherry Williams, Tilman Reitzle
Image Research: Deborah Goodsite, Julia Rubel
Cover design: Peter Koblish, Nancy Sabato

Special thanks are due Marshall Creighton and Dan Henke of the United States Geological
Survey, Bob Sann, Tracie Cayford of the Utah Travel Council, Amy Hastert of the Wisconsin
Department of Tourism, Jay Hammond of the Kentucky Department of Surface Mining, and
Chris Walker of the *Emporia Gazette*.

For photo credits, see p. 144.

Library of Congress Cataloging-in-Publication Data
Rubel, David.
Scholastic atlas of the United States/by David Rubel.
p. cm.—(Scholastic Reference)
Includes index and glossary.
Summary: Maps of each state in the United States, organized by region, accompanied by
facts and figures.
ISBN 0-439-47436-1
1. United States—Maps for children. 2. Children's atlases.   99-26960
[1. United States—Maps. 2. Atlases.] I. Title. II. Series.   CIP
G1200.R8 2000 <G&M>   MAPS
912.73—DC21

10 9 8 7 6 5   03 04 05/06 07

Printed in Mexico
First trade paperback printing, June 2003

Contents

LEGEND
The legend printed above each map explains the meaning of its symbols, colors, and patterns. The legend also contains a scale, which shows the relationship of map distances to actual distances.

STATE NAME ORIGIN
Above the name of each state is an explanation of that name's origin.

STATE FLAG
Below the name of each state is a picture of that state's flag.

STATE LOCATOR MAP
This map shows the location of each state in relation to other continental states.

LEGEND

Interstate Highways · State Capital · Native American Reservations · National Forests · National Parks and Refuges · Highest Point · miles / kilometers

DID YOU KNOW? that Lake Superior is the largest body of freshwater in the world?

The Motor City
The U.S. auto industry began in Detroit and the nearby cities of Dearborn, Flint, and Lansing. When Americans began buying more foreign cars during the 1980s, the auto plants in and around Detroit suffered. Yet the area remains home to America's three largest car companies.

— 400 miles (644 km) —

ABOUT MICHIGAN

NICKNAME: Wolverine State
CAPITAL: Lansing
STATEHOOD: January 26, 1837 (26th)
MOTTO: If you seek a beautiful peninsula, look around you.

POPULATION: 9,990,817 (8th)
AREA: 96,705 sq. mi. (11th) (250,358 sq km)
HIGHEST POINT: 1,979 ft. (Mount Arvon)
LOWEST POINT: 571 ft. (Lake Erie)

FLOWER: Apple blossom
TREE: White pine
BIRD: Robin
FISH: Brook trout

FROM THE OJIBWA WORDS *MICI GAMA*, MEANING "GREAT WATER."

Michigan

A peninsula is a spit of land, shaped like a tongue, bounded on three sides by water. The state of Michigan is actually a pair of peninsulas, one divided from the other by the Straits of Mackinac (pronounced MACK-i-naw). Michigan's sometimes hilly, sometimes swampy Upper Peninsula is connected to the flatter, mitten-shaped Lower Peninsula by the Mackinac Bridge.

Michigan is called the Great Lakes State because it borders four of the five Great Lakes. As a result, shipping has always been an important business there. The locks at Sault Ste. Marie (nicknamed "the Soo") were opened in 1855 to service ships carrying timber and iron ore from Minnesota and the Upper Peninsula. These locks, which equalize the water level between Lake Superior and Lake Huron, are still among the world's busiest.

Michiganders in great numbers also use the Great Lakes for recreation. The rural Upper Peninsula doesn't have many people, but most of them fish. So do the carloads of Detroiters and Chicagoans who visit the Upper Peninsula each summer for a vacation out-of-doors. Despite the fact that it contains every one of Michigan's major cities and important industrial centers, the Lower Peninsula is no less outdoorsy. In fact, Michiganders of both peninsulas own more boats than residents of any other state.

The fish boil has been a Great Lakes tradition since the nineteenth century. It was devised by Scandinavian immigrants who wanted an easy way to cook whitefish and lake trout. For a traditional outdoor fish boil, Michiganders cook chunks of fish, potatoes, and onions in seasoned water over large wood fires.

75%

Michigan's Slice of the Pie
Michigan produces about 75 percent of the sour pie cherries grown in the United States. The area around Traverse City is particularly good for growing cherries because Lake Michigan moderates the weather there, tempering the frosts and cooling the orchards during summer.

Large ships haul cargo from the Midwest to the East (and beyond) using the St. Lawrence Seaway. This system of canals, locks, and dams joins the Great Lakes to the Atlantic Ocean.

STATE FACTS
This box lists useful information about each state. The numbers in parentheses refer to that state's rank among the fifty states. *Statehood* refers to the date that a state joined the Union. The population figures, provided by the Bureau of the Census, are estimates as of July 1, 2001 (the most recent estimates can be found online at www.census.gov).

Key to Metric Abbreviations

cm	centimeters
ha	hectares
kg	kilograms
km	kilometers
l	liters
m	meters
sq km	square kilometers

How to Use This Book

There are certain questions that an atlas can answer easily. For example: What's the capital of Kansas? Or: Which interstate highway runs between San Francisco and Los Angeles? The type of maps used in the *Scholastic Atlas of the United States* present this sort of information well. However, people often ask questions about the United States that maps can't answer. For instance: How are North Carolinians different from South Carolinians? Or: What makes Minnesotans special?

To answer these much more difficult questions, people usually turn to novelists, playwrights, and humorists, rather than mapmakers. Even so, there are facts about each state—who lives in it, what the people do, what the land is like—that can help students understand more about the quality of life there. You'll find many of these facts in the pages that follow, some presented in words and others in pictures. Perhaps not all your questions will be answered, but the description of each state provided will give you a good start.

One final note: The statistics presented in this book are the most recent that were available when the book was updated in 2002. Most reflect data from 2000 and 2001.

CANADA

Maine
page 12

KENNEBEC RIVER

PENOBSCOT RIVER

Vermont
page 20

CONNECTICUT RIVER

MERRIMACK RIVER

New Hampshire
page 16

Massachusetts
page 14

HOUSATONIC RIVER

Rhode Island
page 18

Connecticut
page 10

ATLANTIC OCEAN

New England

The Appalachian
Mountain chain, which
runs from Alabama all the
way north to Canada, dominates the
topography of New England. Among other
ranges, the Appalachians include the Green
Mountains of Vermont, the White Mountains of
New Hampshire, and the Longfellow Mountains of
Maine. The region's most important waterway is
the Connecticut River, whose valley separates the
Western New England Uplands from the slightly
less hilly Eastern New England Uplands.

🛡 20 Interstate Highways   ✪ State Capital   ▲ Highest Point

0	miles	25
0	kilometers	40

The Insurance City

The U.S. insurance industry, which began in Connecticut, has been headquartered in Hartford for more than two hundred years. During the eighteenth century, Hartford firms insured ships and cargoes. Later, they pioneered other types of coverage, such as accident and automobile insurance.

MASSACHUSETTS

Springfield

LITCHFIELD HILLS

HOUSATONIC RIVER

SHEPAUG RIVER

NAUGATUCK RIVER

WILLIMANTIC R.

Putnam

91

84

Windsor

Torrington

Hartford ✪

Manchester

384

Willimantic

SHETUCKET R.

QUINEBAUG RIVER

RHODE ISLAND

Poughkeepsie

New Britain

84

91

Middletown

Norwich

39 5

NEW YORK

691

Meriden

CONNECTICUT R.

THAMES R.

95

Waterbury

84

91

Candlewood Lake

New London

Mystic

Lake Gaillard

New Haven

Danbury

West Haven

95

Groton

684

Stratford

Milford

Long Island Sound

Bridgeport 95

Norwalk

Stamford

Greenwich

287

New York City

ATLANTIC OCEAN

DID YOU KNOW?

that Hartford resident Mark Twain once said of the state's changeable climate, "If you don't like Connecticut weather, wait a minute"?

◄———— 90 miles (145 km) ————►

ABOUT CONNECTICUT

NICKNAME: Constitution State

CAPITAL: Hartford

STATEHOOD: January 9, 1788 (5th)

MOTTO: He who transplanted sustains.

POPULATION: 3,425,074 (29th)

AREA: 5,544 sq. mi. (48th)
(14,353 sq km)

HIGHEST POINT: 2,380 ft. (Mount Frissell)

LOWEST POINT: Sea level (Long Island Sound)

FLOWER: Mountain laurel

TREE: White oak

BIRD: American robin

Connecticut

Today, most people think of Yankees as baseball players. However, when novelist Mark Twain wrote *A Connecticut Yankee in King Arthur's Court* in 1889, he used the word *Yankee* to mean "someone from New England."

Connecticut Yankees were, for Twain, a special breed: They were tinkerers with a knack for making things. Because Connecticut can claim no oil or mineral wealth, residents have had to rely on "Yankee ingenuity" for their prosperity. Products invented in Connecticut include the revolver (by Samuel Colt in 1835), vulcanized rubber (by Charles Goodyear in 1839), and the cylinder lock (by Linus Yale in 1861). Even today, manufacturing is a crucial part of the state's economic success, especially the production of military transport equipment. Factories in Bridgeport turn out helicopters (invented in Connecticut in 1939), while highly skilled workers assemble jet engines in East Hartford and nuclear submarines in Groton.

Although the Connecticut River Valley is quite fertile, the thin, rocky soil on either side of it makes farming elsewhere in Connecticut difficult. To the west of the river, the land rises into the Litchfield Hills, where the state's highest elevations are found. On the other side of the Connecticut River, the land slopes down to the southeast. Along the state's southern border are marshy coastal lowlands that drain into Long Island Sound. This coastal plain and the Connecticut River Valley, both relatively flat, hold most of Connecticut's larger cities.

Native American Gaming
Although gambling is generally illegal in Connecticut, the state contains two of the world's largest casinos: the Mohegan Sun and Foxwoods, both near New London. These casinos are allowed to operate because they belong to Native American groups, which are treated legally as independent nations existing within the United States.

Wrap It Up
What little agriculture Connecticut does have involves mostly direct-to-market products, such as flowering plants, fresh vegetables, and Christmas trees. The one important exception is shade-grown tobacco leaf. The best Connecticut River Valley leaves, about twenty-four inches (61 cm) long, are used to wrap cigars.

Judging by per-capita income, Connecticut is the nation's richest state. Its wealthiest area, Fairfield County, nearly borders New York City. Residents there include many well-paid corporate executives who commute to jobs in Manhattan.

LEGEND

Interstate Highways	State Capital	National Parks and Refuges	National Forests	Highest Point	0 miles 50 / 0 kilometers 80

Parlez Vous?

There are no minorities to speak of in Maine, which is 98 percent white. However, many of those whites are transplanted French Canadians for whom English is a second language. Much of Maine is bilingual, and in the St. John River Valley, French is the dominant tongue.

DID YOU KNOW?

that the 2,034-mile-long (3,273-kilometer-long) Appalachian Trail ends at Mount Katahdin, Maine's highest point? Because of its height, Mount Katahdin is also the first place that the sun strikes the continental United States.

← 207 miles (333 km) →

ABOUT MAINE

NICKNAME: Pine Tree State
CAPITAL: Augusta
STATEHOOD: March 15, 1820 (23rd)
MOTTO: I direct.

POPULATION: 1,286,670 (40th)
AREA: 35,387 sq. mi. (39th)
(91,613 sq km)
HIGHEST POINT: 5,267 ft. (Mount Katahdin)
LOWEST POINT: Sea level (Atlantic Ocean)

FLOWER: White pinecone and tassel
TREE: White pine
BIRD: Chickadee
FISH: Landlocked salmon

Maine

Maine is large, with about as much land as the rest of New England combined. It's also roomy, with a population only slightly larger than that of Rhode Island. In fact, Maine is the least densely populated state east of the Mississippi River. This is especially true north of Bangor, where the terrain becomes mountainous, heavily forested, and sometimes impassable.

That's why most Mainers live in towns along one of the state's tidal rivers or in fishing villages along the Atlantic coast. In the north, many Mainers earn their livings from the timber industry, while in the south, tourism pays a large share of the bills. The southern coast from Kittery to Casco Bay is particularly popular with vacationers, who rent houses during the summer to enjoy Maine's scenic beauty and cool temperatures. (The ocean water is usually too cold for swimming.)

Beyond their skill at trapping lobsters, native Mainers are also celebrated for their industriousness and endurance. Their state's environment is harsh, with long bitter winters and a challenging landscape. Yet, since the first English settlers landed in 1607, the people of Maine have shown remarkable perseverance in response to these environmental challenges. As a result, they have achieved a national cultural importance far beyond their economic and political status.

Maine's generally poor soil supports very little agriculture. That's not the case in Aroostook County, however, where potato farms compete with those in Idaho. Income from potatoes is so important to northeastern Maine that schools regularly excuse students so they can help out with the fall harvest.

Maine's Annual Lobster Catch

$180 Million
$150 Million
$120 Million
$90 Million

1995 1996 1997 1998 1999 2000

Fishing has long been an important part of the Maine economy, and lobsters, which flourish in the state's cool coastal waters, remain the most valuable catch. However, rising prices have encouraged overfishing, and ecologists now worry that the future of the Maine lobster could be threatened.

During the last Ice Age, glaciers carved Maine's rocky shoreline into scenic cliffs, bays, coves, and beaches. Maine's numerous offshore islands are mostly the tops of hills submerged when those glaciers melted and the sea level rose.

LEGEND

Interstate Highways	**State Capital**	**National Parks and Refuges**
Marshlands	**Highest Point**	

```
0        miles        25
0      kilometers     40
```

DID YOU KNOW?

that there's a Lake Chargoggagoggmanchauggauggag-oggchaubunagungamaugg near Worcester? This Native American name means "You fish on your side; I fish on my side; nobody fishes in the middle."

VERMONT

NEW HAMPSHIRE

• Manchester

• Bennington

N.Y.

Williamstown •
North Adams •
•field

DEERFIELD R.

CONNECTICUT RIVER

Fitchburg •
Leominster •

Haverhill •
Lawrence •

MERRIMACK R.

Gloucester •

ATLANTIC OCEAN

Quabbin Reservoir

Amherst •

Northampton •

BERKSHIRE HILLS

HOUSATONIC R.

Holyoke •

Springfield

Wachusett Reservoir

Worcester •

Milford •

Webster •

Lowell

Lexington •

Peabody •

Salem •

Cambridge •

Newton •

Framingham •

★ **Boston**

Quincy •

Brockton •

Plymouth •

CHARLES R.

Massachusetts Bay

Cape Cod National Seashore

Provincetown •

Cape Cod Bay

CONNECTICUT

Providence •

RHODE ISLAND

TAUNTON R.

Assawompset Pond

Fall River •
New Bedford •

Hyannis •

Falmouth •

Nantucket Sound

Oak Bluffs •

Martha's Vineyard

Nantucket Island

The Cultural Berkshires

Many prominent music and dance groups perform in the Berkshires during the summer. The Boston Symphony Orchestra, for example, has been performing at Tanglewood, near Lenox, since 1936. In nearby Lee, the Jacob's Pillow Dance Festival features traditional and modern dance as well as ballet.

190 miles (306 km)

ABOUT MASSACHUSETTS

NICKNAME: Bay State

CAPITAL: Boston

STATEHOOD: February 6, 1788 (6th)

MOTTO: By the sword we seek peace, but peace only under liberty.

POPULATION: 6,379,304 (13th)

AREA: 10,555 sq. mi. (44th) (27,326 sq km)

HIGHEST POINT: 3,487 ft. (Mount Greylock)

LOWEST POINT: Sea level (Atlantic Ocean)

FLOWER: Mayflower

TREE: American elm

BIRD: Chickadee

FISH: Cod

New England • Massachusetts

14

Massachusetts

When people talk about the United States as a "melting pot" of many different cultures, Massachusetts provides a ready example. Although Yankee Protestants dominated the colony for two hundred years, the textile mills that opened near Boston during the nineteenth century attracted a flood of immigrants. First came the Irish, then the French Canadians, then the Italians and other Europeans. The textile mills are gone now, but Massachusetts remains a top manufacturing state, with a population that's still ethnically diverse.

New Bedford, for example, contains the largest community of Portuguese Americans. The great-great-grandfathers of these people came to America to work in the whaling industry. Now many of their descendants work as commercial fishermen and in fish-processing plants. On the other hand, Boston is predominantly Irish, famous for its long string of Irish mayors. Of course, it's also the financial capital of New England, as well as the region's population center. Massachusetts has nearly as many residents as the other five New England states combined, and half of these people live in the Boston area.

Along with the rest of the Massachusetts coastline, Boston sits on the sandy Atlantic Coastal Plain. Inland, the land rises slowly into the rocky New England Uplands. The fertile Connecticut River Valley, which divides the state, separates the southern fringe of the White Mountains (in the east) from the Berkshire Hills (in the west).

Silicon Valley East
Among the most successful businesses in Massachusetts are the technology firms lining Route 128 west of Boston. These companies have taken particular advantage of the high-tech workforce being created by such local (yet nationally prominent) universities as Harvard and the Massachusetts Institute of Technology.

End of the Line
Cape Cod, a sandy peninsula sixty-five miles (105 km) long, is what geologists call a terminal moraine. It marks the farthest point reached by the glacier that carved out the Connecticut River Valley. It's also the line along which the melting glacier deposited all the rocky debris it had been carrying.

Cranberries grow in bogs, or areas of wet spongy ground, that are usually flooded at harvesttime. Although the state's generally poor soil supports little agriculture, the cranberry bogs of southeastern Massachusetts produce nearly 40 percent of the nation's crop.

15

Interstate Highways

State Capital

National Parks and Refuges

National Forests

Highest Point

| 0 | miles | 25 |
| 0 | miles | 40 |

Although most people think of New Hampshire as primarily rural, it contains significant manufacturing. The most heavily industrialized area is Manchester, New Hampshire's largest city, where factories make machinery, computers, military communications equipment, and plastics.

DID YOU KNOW?

that New Hampshire's state representatives, who are paid just one hundred dollars a year, haven't gotten a raise since 1784?

CANADA

HALLS STREAM

Connecticut Lakes

ANDROSCOGGIN R.

Umbagog Lake

Berlin

St. Johnsbury

Littleton

WHITE MOUNTAINS

MAINE

93

Conway

VERMONT

Plymouth

Squam Lake

Newfound Lake

Lake Winnipesaukee

Hanover

Lebanon

Laconia

Franklin

Portland

Great East Lake

SALMON FALLS RIVER

Sunapee Lake

89

Rochester

Claremont

MERRIMACK RIVER

Dover

PISCATAQUA RIVER

CONNECTICUT RIVER

★ **Concord**

93

Portsmouth

Manchester

Exeter

95

Keene

Derry

EXETER RIVER

ATLANTIC OCEAN

Brattleboro

Wapack National Wildlife Refuge

Nashua

93

MASSACHUSETTS

Lowell

93 miles (150 km)

ABOUT NEW HAMPSHIRE

NICKNAME: Granite State

CAPITAL: Concord

STATEHOOD: June 21, 1788 (9th)

MOTTO: Live free or die.

POPULATION: 1,259,181 (41st)

AREA: 9,351 sq. mi. (46th)
(24,209 sq km)

HIGHEST POINT: 6,288 ft. (Mount Washington)

LOWEST POINT: Sea level (Atlantic Ocean)

FLOWER: Purple lilac

TREE: White birch

BIRD: Purple finch

FISH: Brook trout, striped bass

New Hampshire

More than most Americans, the residents of New Hampshire honor the country's past and attempt to preserve older visions of the way people's lives should be run. Citizens of other states typically have little contact with their local governments, yet towns in New Hampshire still hold open meetings to decide important public issues. In general, the people of New Hampshire believe strongly in exercising their political voices, and this is particularly true every four years when the state hosts its traditional "first in the nation" presidential primary.

In northern New Hampshire, where the stony White Mountains dominate the landscape, most people live in small towns that depend on lumber for their livelihood. Like Connecticut, it's a place of enduring Yankee values, where the highly conservative residents (nearly all of whom are white) are often compared to the granite bedrock underlying the state. The only industrial center is Berlin, where large mills process trees into paper and wood pulp.

South of the White Mountains, however, New Hampshire contains a number of large urban centers that house about 85 percent of the state's population. People originally concentrated in these cities because southern New Hampshire is highly industrialized. Lately, however, more and more people have been moving from Boston to suburban New Hampshire to escape the city and Massachusetts state taxes. New Hampshire has neither an income tax nor a sales tax.

Every year on the first Tuesday in March, citizens of New Hampshire take part in a tradition dating back to colonial times: the town meeting. Before the spring thaw comes and mud makes some roads impassable, town residents gather to vote on school budgets, property taxes, and other government matters.

Top Wind Speed: 231 miles per hour (372 km/hr)

The Windiest Place on Earth
Atop Mount Washington, the highest peak in New England, the National Weather Service operates a climate research station. On April 12, 1934, this station's instruments registered a world-record wind speed of 231 miles per hour. Normally, winter gusts on Mount Washington range from 120 to 160 miles (193 to 257 km) per hour.

In a Native American language once spoken in New Hampshire, *monadnock* means "mountain that stands alone." More recently, Mount Monadnock near Keene has given its name to isolated plugs of granite that become mountains once the surrounding land has eroded away.

17

LEGEND

🛣 **20** Interstate Highways

✪ State Capital

⬜ Native American Reservations

⬛ National Parks and Refuges

▦ Marshlands

▲ Highest Point

| 0 | miles | 10 |
| 0 | kilometers | 16 |

MASSACHUSETTS

Woonsocket

Pascoag

Central Falls

Pawtucket

SEEKONK RIVER

East Providence

Scituate Reservoir

▲

Providence ✪

Cranston

PROVIDENCE R.

195

Barrington

Fall River

Warwick

West Warwick

Bristol

Narragansett Bay

Prudence Island

Tiverton

SAKONNET R.

Conanicut Island

Rhode Island

QUEEN RIVER

Kingston

Newport

Narragansett Reservation

Worden Pond

PAWCATUCK RIVER

Westerly

Watchaug Pond

Trustom Pond National Wildlife Refuge

Block Island Sound

Block Island

ATLANTIC OCEAN

CONNECTICUT

BLACKSTONE R.

95

295

95

95

95

PAWTUXET R.

During the late nineteenth century, Newport was perhaps the world's most fashionable resort. The richest Americans built summer "cottages" there along the famous Newport Cliff Walk. The grandest of these mansions is the seventy-room Breakers, built by the Vanderbilt family in 1892.

DID YOU KNOW?

that New Jersey is the only state more densely populated than Rhode Island?

← 37 miles (60 km) →

ABOUT RHODE ISLAND

NICKNAME: Ocean State

CAPITAL: Providence

STATEHOOD: May 29, 1790 (13th)

MOTTO: Hope.

POPULATION: 1,058,920 (43rd)

AREA: 1,545 sq. mi. (50th) (4,000 sq km)

HIGHEST POINT: 812 ft. (Jerimoth Hill)

LOWEST POINT: Sea level (Atlantic Ocean)

FLOWER: Violet

TREE: Red maple

BIRD: Rhode Island red (chicken)

Rhode Island

Because Rhode Island is the smallest state, it's particularly easy for Rhode Islanders to travel—that is, they don't have to go very far to reach Massachusetts or Connecticut. Yet people there will tell you that Rhode Islanders like to stay close to home. Part of the reason is that they're proud of where they live, even though there's so little of it.

Since the founding of the colony by Protestant dissidents in 1636, Rhode Islanders have championed religious tolerance. Those who have benefited include Jews, who in 1763 established the first synagogue in the colonies in Newport, and Roman Catholics, who immigrated to the state in large numbers once Rhode Island began to industrialize during the nineteenth century.

The state had little choice but to industrialize. Because of its poor soil, agriculture wasn't an option. So, relying on their reputation for fine craftsmanship, Rhode Islanders built factories instead. These factories, in turn, attracted workers from other countries who diversified the mostly white, mostly Protestant population. Today, Rhode Island has a higher percentage of Roman Catholics than any other state, with large Irish and Italian communities in Providence and French Canadians in Woonsocket.

The island for which the state is named is the largest of thirty-five in Narragansett Bay, where sand beaches and salt marshes dominate the terrain. On the mainland, however, the lowlands of the Atlantic Coastal Plain quickly give way to the low, rocky hills of the New England Uplands.

Factories in Providence began making costume jewelry in 1794, and the city remains a national leader in the field. Designed to be trendy and disposable, these fashion accessories are affordable because they're made from inexpensive materials rather than precious metals and gemstones.

A Tiny Fraction of the Size
Rhode Island is so small that it would take 425 Rhode Islands to fill up just one Alaska, the largest of the fifty states.

Although freighters use it to reach the busy port of Providence, Narragansett Bay is best known for its water sports. In particular, it's the focus of yachting on the Atlantic coast.

CANADA

Lake Memphremagog

MISSISQUOI R.

Newport

St. Albans

Lake Champlain

Plattsburgh

LAMOILLE RIVER

BLACK RIVER

Seymour Lake

Granby

91

GREEN MOUNTAINS

Burlington

Waterbury

St. Johnsbury

93

DID YOU KNOW?

that Vermont has more than one hundred covered bridges, most constructed before 1912 and all protected by law?

Montpelier ⭐

WINOOSKI RIVER

Vergennes

Barre

Middlebury

89

GREEN MOUNTAINS

OTTER CREEK

WHITE RIVER

CONNECTICUT RIVER

91

NEW YORK

Rutland

METTAWEE RIVER

NEW HAMPSHIRE

91

Vermont has short, cool summers and long, snowy winters, making it a favorite spot for skiing. The first Green Mountain ski areas opened in the 1930s, but resorts such as Mount Snow, Stratton, Stowe, and Killington didn't become popular until the 1960s.

WEST RIVER

Bennington

Keene

Brattleboro

Albany

MASS.

◄———— 90 miles (145 km) ————►

ABOUT VERMONT

NICKNAME: Green Mountain State

CAPITAL: Montpelier

STATEHOOD: March 4, 1791 (14th)

MOTTO: Freedom and unity.

POPULATION: 613,090 (49th)

AREA: 9,615 sq. mi. (45th)
(24,892 sq km)

HIGHEST POINT: 4,393 ft. (Mount Mansfield)

LOWEST POINT: 95 ft. (Lake Champlain)

FLOWER: Red clover

TREE: Sugar maple

BIRD: Hermit thrush

FISH: Brook trout, walleye pike

Vermont

Vermont is a small-town state. Montpelier, the smallest state capital, contains just eight thousand residents, and Vermont's other cities aren't much larger. In fact, about as many people live in Boston as live in all of Vermont. Even the factories there are small: Four out of five employ fewer than fifty people.

As late as the 1950s, the typical Vermonter was a Protestant of English descent, and the state is still 99 percent white. Following the social upheaval of the 1960s, however, many young people moved to Vermont, hoping for a simpler, more natural lifestyle. One result of this influx (and the new sensibility brought by these people) has been the development of a new economically important specialty foods market in the state. Products such as goat cheese, organic vegetables, and emu burgers now proudly bear the "Made in Vermont" label and sell nationwide.

Like its neighbors, Vermont is mountainous; yet unlike the other New England states, Vermont depends heavily on agriculture. Crops aren't very profitable, because only the Connecticut River Valley has suitable soil, so most Vermont farmers raise livestock instead. Dairy cows happily graze on most mountainsides, producing the milk used to make Vermont's famous cheddar cheese.

The heavily forested Green Mountains that give Vermont its name are the backbone of the state, running north to south in a band about thirty miles (50 km) wide. The rest of the state is mostly hill country cut by fast-flowing streams.

Milk accounts for about two thirds of Vermont's farm income. Traditionally, that milk has gone to make cheddar cheese. However, some of it now goes to the Ben & Jerry's ice cream factory in Waterbury. With flavors such as Rainforest Crunch and Cherry Garcia, founders Ben Cohen and Jerry Greenfield have used 1960s sensibilities to promote their product.

Vermont leads the nation in maple syrup production, which the locals call sugaring. Maple sap begins to flow in early spring, when daytime temperatures first rise above 40°F (5°C) yet nighttime temperatures remain below freezing. Sugarmakers boil down the sap from four trees, about forty gallons (150 l), to make a single gallon (3.8 l) of syrup.

Poet Robert Frost once described fall in the Green Mountains as a time when the "leaves go to glory." About three out of every four Vermonters live either on farms or in small towns like this one.

CANADA

LAKE ONTARIO

New York
page 30

ERIE CANAL

MOHAWK RIVER

LAKE ERIE

ALLEGHENY RIVER

HUDSON RIVER

OHIO RIVER

Pennsylvania
page 32

SUSQUEHANNA RIVER

DELAWARE RIVER

New
Jersey
page 28

MONONGAHELA RIVER

POTOMAC RIVER

Maryland
page 26

Delaware
page 24

Washington,
D.C.
page 34

ATLANTIC OCEAN

Every Mid-Atlantic state sits—at least in some small part—on both the Piedmont Plateau and the Atlantic Coastal Plain. The line along which these two regions meet is called the fall line because the land there drops sharply. Two hundred years ago, George Washington chose the point at which the fall line crosses the Potomac River for the location of his new federal city. Hikers today can easily tell when they're near the fall line because of all the rapids and waterfalls it creates.

Mid-Atlantic

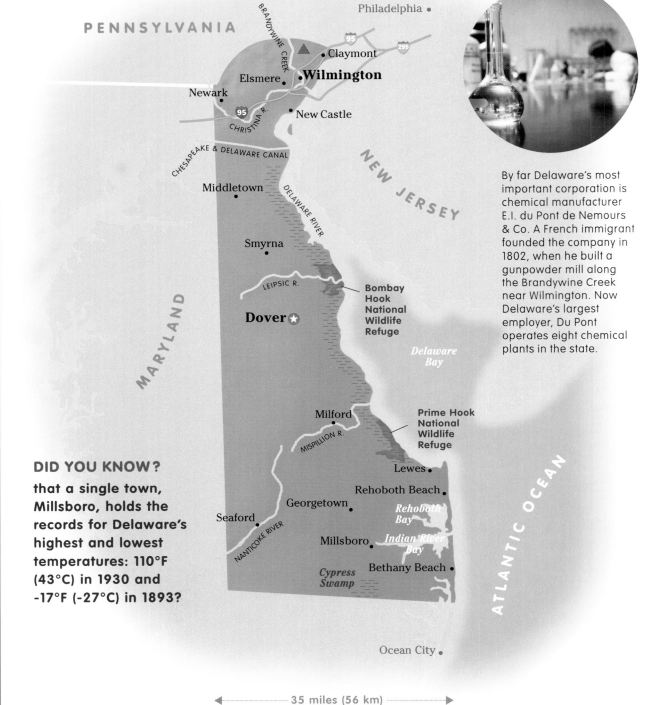

PENNSYLVANIA

Philadelphia

BRANDYWINE CREEK

95

295

Claymont

Wilmington

Elsmere

Newark

95

New Castle

CHRISTINA R.

CHESAPEAKE & DELAWARE CANAL

NEW JERSEY

Middletown

DELAWARE RIVER

Smyrna

LEIPSIC R.

Bombay Hook National Wildlife Refuge

Dover ⭐

Delaware Bay

MARYLAND

Milford

MISPILLION R.

Prime Hook National Wildlife Refuge

Lewes

Rehoboth Beach

Georgetown

Rehoboth Bay

Seaford

Millsboro

Indian River Bay

NANTICOKE RIVER

Bethany Beach

Cypress Swamp

ATLANTIC OCEAN

Ocean City

By far Delaware's most important corporation is chemical manufacturer E.I. du Pont de Nemours & Co. A French immigrant founded the company in 1802, when he built a gunpowder mill along the Brandywine Creek near Wilmington. Now Delaware's largest employer, Du Pont operates eight chemical plants in the state.

DID YOU KNOW?

that a single town, Millsboro, holds the records for Delaware's highest and lowest temperatures: 110°F (43°C) in 1930 and -17°F (-27°C) in 1893?

← 35 miles (56 km) →

ABOUT DELAWARE

NICKNAME: First State

CAPITAL: Dover

STATEHOOD: December 7, 1787 (1st)

MOTTO: Liberty and independence.

POPULATION: 796,165 (45th)

AREA: 2,489 sq. mi. (49th)
(6,444 sq km)

HIGHEST POINT: 448 ft. (Ebright Road)

LOWEST POINT: Sea level (Atlantic Ocean)

FLOWER: Peach blossom

TREE: American holly

BIRD: Blue hen chicken

FISH: Weakfish

Delaware

DECEMBER 7, 1787

In Delaware, everyone seems to know everyone else. Of course that's not literally true, yet the state is small enough that its residents cross paths often. Because of this, Delaware is the sort of place where much business gets done in restaurants and at social gatherings.

After chemicals—that is, after Du Pont—Delaware's biggest business is incorporation. Of the five hundred largest U.S. companies, more than half are Delaware corporations. This may seem odd for such a small state, but Delaware has been passing laws to attract corporations since 1899. Although nearly all of these companies do business elsewhere, they've incorporated in Delaware because of the state's low taxation, up-to-date laws, and experienced judges. In return, they provide work for armies of lawyers, accountants, and other business professionals familiar with the state's legal requirements and procedures. Overall, corporate taxes and fees make up more than one fifth of Delaware's total revenue.

Delaware sits on the Delmarva Peninsula, which separates the Chesapeake Bay from the Atlantic Ocean. The Chesapeake & Delaware Canal, linking these two bodies of water, provides an important boundary between the state's industrial north and its agricultural south. Northern Delaware contains about two thirds of the state's population and all of its major transportation routes, while the main industry in the south is chicken farming.

The Brandywine Valley north of Wilmington is called Chateau Country because of its many Du Pont family mansions. Two have become museums: Winterthur (pictured above) houses the nation's finest collection of early American decorative arts, while the Hagley Museum, on the site of the original Du Pont powder works, documents life during the nineteenth century.

PENNSYLVANIA

12 mi (19 km)

New Castle

M.D.

NEW JERSEY

Delaware is the only state with a partially rounded border, the result of a land dispute during the early 1680s. At that time, William Penn and the Duke of York agreed that the boundary between Pennsylvania and Delaware would be an arc "drawn at twelve miles' distance from New Castle."

The salt marshes and estuaries that line Delaware Bay provide excellent habitats for birds and shellfish. Delaware's strict shoreline protection laws, the first of their kind in the nation, forbid pollution-causing factories too close to the bay.

LEGEND

🛣 **20** Interstate Highways

⊛ State Capital

■ National Parks and Refuges

▒ Marshlands

▲ Highest Point

```
0        miles      25
0     kilometers    40
```

DID YOU KNOW?

that a Baltimore law makes it illegal to take a lion to the movies?

PENNSYLVANIA

Philadelphia •

SUSQUEHANNA R.

Wilmington •

68 Cumberland • Hagerstown • Westminster • Bel Air • Aberdeen Elkton •

Deep Creek Lake

ALLEGHENY MOUNTAINS

70

81

Frederick • Liberty Reservoir **83**

95

POTOMAC RIVER

70 **Baltimore**

WEST VIRGINIA

270 Columbia • Dundalk • CHESTER R.

Wheaton • **95**

Rockville • Silver Spring • **97**

DELAWARE

VIRGINIA

Washington, D.C. • Bowie • **Annapolis** ⊛

Easton • Blackwater National Wildlife Refuge

95

CHOPTANK R.

Cambridge •

NANTICOKE R.

PATUXENT RIVER

Salisbury • Ocean City •

Chesapeake Bay

• Richmond

Assateague Island National Seashore

ATLANTIC OCEAN

During the late 1980s, Baltimore energetically renovated its downtown Inner Harbor area. The centerpiece was a hundred-million-dollar ballpark: Oriole Park at Camden Yards. The success of this old-style brick baseball stadium—nearly every game is sold out—has inspired other cities, such as Detroit and San Francisco, to build their own downtown ballparks.

195 miles (314 km)

ABOUT MARYLAND

NICKNAME: Old Line State

CAPITAL: Annapolis

STATEHOOD: April 28, 1788 (7th)

MOTTO: Manly deeds, womanly words.

POPULATION: 5,375,156 (19th)

AREA: 12,407 sq. mi. (42nd) (32,120 sq km)

HIGHEST POINT: 3,360 ft. (Backbone Mt.)

LOWEST POINT: Sea level (Atlantic Ocean)

FLOWER: Black-eyed Susan

TREE: White oak

BIRD: Baltimore oriole

FISH: Rockfish

Maryland

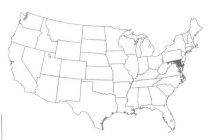

Maryland has so many different looks that what you see depends on what you're looking for. If you're looking for people, you'll find most of them living between Washington, D.C., and Baltimore. Three out of every four Marylanders live in this densely populated corridor because most of the jobs are there. The leading industries are electrical equipment and food processing, but the federal government is also a major employer. Many Marylanders commute to jobs in D.C., but even more work at federal facilities in Maryland.

If you're looking for land, you'll find that most of the state is rural. On Maryland's Eastern Shore, part of the Atlantic Coastal Plain, farmers raise broiler chickens inland while resort towns line the Atlantic beaches. In western Maryland, atop the hilly Piedmont, fertile farmland is occasionally interrupted by large belts of clay. (This clay provided the raw material for the bricks that have made Maryland's homes and factories so distinctive.) Farther west, in the section of the state called the "bird's wing" because of its odd shape, the land rises sharply into the Allegheny Mountains.

Finally, even if you're not looking for water, you'll find it impossible to miss Chesapeake Bay, the largest estuary in the United States. The bay was formed at the end of the last Ice Age when rising seawater flooded the southern Susquehanna River Valley. Today, the bay is 193 miles (311 km) long with 3,200 miles (5,200 km) of shoreline.

Maryland's older industrial look often appeals to feature-film makers in search of colorful urban locations. Among the first directors to shoot films in Baltimore were home-grown talents Barry Levinson (*Diner, Avalon*) and John Waters (*Hairspray, Cry-Baby*). The city now expects to host two or three major productions each year.

1795   1995

Shifting Shoreline
Maryland's shoreline has been frustrating mapmakers for centuries. The problem is that the tidal waters of Chesapeake Bay keep rearranging the land, filling in swamps as they wash away islands.

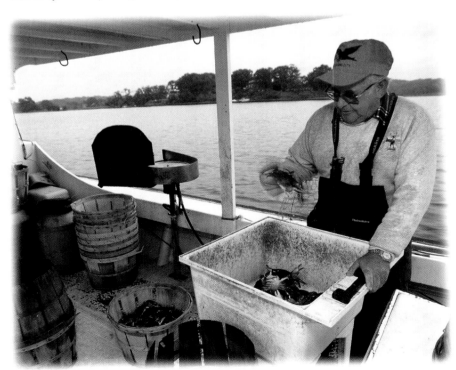

Although pollution and overfishing have dramatically reduced the oyster and striped bass populations, Chesapeake Bay still produces about one hundred million pounds (45 million kg) of seafood each year, including fifty million pounds (23 million kg) of blue crab.

LEGEND

Interstate Highways · State Capital · National Parks and Refuges · Marshlands · Highest Point

| 0 | | miles | 25 |
| 0 | | kilometers | 40 |

New Jersey has one of the busiest and most extensive transportation systems in the world. The trucking, shipping, and air routes that converge at Newark make use of the New Jersey Turnpike (the busiest U.S. toll road), the Port of Newark, and Newark Airport.

NEW YORK

KITTATINNY MTS.

Greenwood Lake

Wanaque Reservoir

Lake Hopatcong

80

Dover

Paterson

Clifton

Hoboken · New York City

287

Newark

Jersey City

Bayonne

78

Elizabeth

Plainfield

278

Edison

Perth Amboy

DELAWARE RIVER

RARITAN RIVER

Princeton

Red Bank

95

Long Branch

95

⭐ **Trenton**

Asbury Park

PENNSYLVANIA

95

195

295

Philadelphia

New Jersey Turnpike

PINE BARRENS

Garden State Parkway

76

Camden

Cherry Hill

Wilmington

295

ATLANTIC OCEAN

MULLICA RIVER

Vineland

GREAT EGG HARBOR RIVER

Edwin B. Forsythe National Wildlife Refuge

MAURICE RIVER

Atlantic City

DELAWARE

Delaware Bay

Cape May

HUDSON RIVER

95

DID YOU KNOW?

that it's illegal to pump your own gasoline at service stations in New Jersey?

57 miles (92 km)

ABOUT NEW JERSEY

NICKNAME: Garden State
CAPITAL: Trenton
STATEHOOD: December 18, 1787 (3rd)
MOTTO: Liberty and prosperity.

POPULATION: 8,484,431 (9th)
AREA: 8,722 sq. mi. (47th) (22,580 sq km)
HIGHEST POINT: 1,803 ft. (High Point)
LOWEST POINT: Sea level (Atlantic Ocean)

FLOWER: Purple violet
TREE: Red oak
BIRD: Eastern goldfinch

New Jersey

Benjamin Franklin once described New Jersey as "a cider barrel tapped at both ends." He was referring to the fact that in colonial times New Jersey grew much of the food eaten in New York City and Philadelphia. Two centuries later, those cities still influence life in northern and southern New Jersey, respectively. Residents of the state's numerous suburbs often commute to jobs in New York City or Philadelphia, watch television stations emanating from those cities, and root for their major league sports teams.

Yet New Jersey has changed in many other ways. Most notably, it has transformed itself into an industrial powerhouse. For example, New Jersey leads the nation in pharmaceutical drug manufacturing and trails only Texas in chemical production. In addition, New Jersey boasts a number of important industrial research facilities—a tradition begun by Thomas Edison in 1876, when he built the first U.S. research laboratory in Menlo Park. Because of all this heavy industry, New Jersey has paid a steep price in toxic waste and environmental pollution. Recognizing this, a number of communities (especially Newark) have lately begun instituting promising clean-up programs.

Ironically, because so many New Jerseyans live crowded into suburbs, two thirds of the state is open land. In southern and eastern Jersey, this land is dominated by the Pine Barrens, a region of infertile soil sitting atop the Cohansey Aquifer, which is believed to hold the largest supply of freshwater in the Northeast.

The Jersey Shore begins at Cape May, the nation's first summer resort. A short drive north is Atlantic City, the home of the Miss America pageant since 1921 and legalized gambling since 1978. Closer to New York City are the beach towns made famous by Bruce Springsteen, who grew up near Asbury Park.

Among the states, New Jersey has the ninth largest population and the fourth smallest area. This means that a lot of New Jerseyans live in a relatively small space. As a result, New Jersey has the highest population density in the United States, with more people per square mile than India or Japan.

New Jersey's nickname is the Garden State because of its many truck farms. These small farms produce fresh vegetables, milk, and eggs that are shipped by truck to New York City and Philadelphia.

Interstate Highways

State Capital

Native American Reservations

National Forests

Highest Point

0 miles 50
0 kilometers 80

New York City is the hub of many industries, including fashion, theater, art, broadcasting, publishing, advertising, public relations, and financial services. New York City's financial community is collectively known as Wall Street because the New York Stock Exchange is located there.

ST. LAWRENCE RIVER

St. Regis Reservation

CANADA

Ogdensburg
Potsdam
Plattsburgh
Lake Placid
Lake Champlain
Burlington

Watertown

ADIRONDACK MTS.

RAQUETTE R.

87

LAKE ONTARIO

Oswego

81

Oneida Lake
Rome

Great Sacandaga Lake

Lake George

METTAWEE RIVER

ERIE CANAL

NIAGARA R.

Niagara Falls

Rochester

Syracuse

Geneva

Utica

90

MOHAWK RIVER

Glens Falls

Schenectady

Buffalo

90

L. ERIE

GENESEE RIVER

390

Finger Lakes

Ithaca

Oneonta

88

Albany
Troy

VERMONT

MASS.

Cattaraugus Reservation

Corning

81

CATSKILL MTS.

Ashokan Reservoir

HUDSON RIVER

90

Jamestown

Elmira

ALLEGHENY R.

SUSQUEHANNA R.

Binghamton

Kingston

Poughkeepsie

CONN.

Allegany Reservation

DELAWARE R.

87

84

Newburgh
Middletown

PENNSYLVANIA

Scranton

684

95

Long Island Sound

DID YOU KNOW?

that in 1644 the governor of New York (then New Amsterdam) noted eighteen languages being spoken by the colony's inhabitants?

Yonkers

New York City

Levittown
Hempstead

495

Riverhead

Allentown

278

N.J.

ATLANTIC OCEAN

Trenton

320 miles (515 km)

ABOUT NEW YORK

NICKNAME: Empire State	**POPULATION:** 19,011,378 (3rd)	**FLOWER:** Rose
CAPITAL: Albany	**AREA:** 54,471 sq. mi. (27th)	**TREE:** Sugar maple
STATEHOOD: July 26, 1788 (11th)	(141,019 sq km)	**BIRD:** Bluebird
MOTTO: Ever upward.	**HIGHEST POINT:** 5,344 ft. (Mount Marcy)	**FISH:** Brook trout
	LOWEST POINT: Sea level (Atlantic Ocean)	

New York

Until the late 1960s, New York State led the nation in nearly every economic, population, and cultural category. Now it ranks third in population and seventh in manufacturing jobs. New York's economic decline has particularly troubled upstate cities such as Buffalo and Rochester, which have lost thousands of high-paying industrial jobs. On the other hand, New York City remains essentially unchanged: It continues to be an international cultural center, the home of the world's most important financial markets, and the headquarters of more major corporations than anywhere else.

A clear distinction exists between residents of "the City" and the rest of the state's population. Manhattanites tend to think of upstate New York as nearly unpopulated, while many upstaters would probably consider New York City a foreign land if it didn't share the same state government. In fact, a remarkable number of languages are spoken in New York City, which has long been an important point of entry for immigrants.

Just as New York State's people and economy are highly diverse, so is its geography. The only state to border both the Atlantic Ocean and the Great Lakes, New York encompasses nine topographical regions, most created by glaciers during the last Ice Age. The state's two major mountain ranges are the Catskills and the Adirondacks. The Adirondacks are particularly notable because the state has set aside a large portion of these rugged, sparsely populated mountains as a wilderness preserve.

The Melting Pot
Although most cities in New York have varied populations, none compares with New York City for its racial, religious, and ethnic mix. For instance, in New York City, there are significant populations of Puerto Ricans, Dominicans, Haitians, Mexicans, Jews, and Chinese. In addition, there are more blacks in New York than in any other state.

Buffalo gets more attention, but Syracuse is actually the snowiest U.S. city outside Alaska, with a mean annual snowfall of 110.1 inches (279.7 cm). The reason is the lake effect. As air moves west, it soaks up moisture over the Great Lakes. When this air reaches land and cools down, the excess moisture is squeezed out as snow.

In the Hudson River Valley, although apples are an important crop, milk is the leading agricultural commodity. Statewide, dairy products account for about half of all farm income.

LEGEND

🛣 **20** Interstate Highways

✪ State Capital

◼ National Parks and Refuges

🌲 National Forests

▲ Highest Point

0 — miles — 50
0 — kilometers — 80

DID YOU KNOW?

that Pittsburgh's steel factories once produced so much smoke that motorists had to use headlights during the day?

LAKE ERIE

NEW YORK

OHIO

Erie
Erie National Wildlife Refuge
Pymatuning Reservoir
ALLEGHENY RIVER
Oil City
Bradford
Binghamton
DELAWARE RIVER
Lake Wallenpaupack
Scranton
Wilkes-Barre
Williamsport
WEST BRANCH SUSQUEHANNA R.
Youngstown
New Castle
Butler
State College
ALLEGHENY MTS.
Hazleton
Pottsville
Bethlehem
N.J.
Pittsburgh
Johnstown
Altoona
JUNIATA R.
Harrisburg
Hershey
Reading
SCHUYLKILL R.
Allentown
Greensburg
Raystown Lake
Carlisle
Lancaster
SUSQUEHANNA R.
Trenton
OHIO R.
MONONGAHELA R.
Chambersburg
York
Philadelphia
Chester
Wilmington
W. VA.
VA.
MARYLAND
Baltimore
DEL.

Lancaster County in the heart of Pennsylvania Dutch country has a high concentration of dairy farms. That's why Milton Hershey chose to locate his milk chocolate business there. Since Hershey's factory opened in 1905, it has grown to become the world's largest chocolate plant.

◄—————— 307 miles (494 km) ——————►

ABOUT PENNSYLVANIA

NICKNAME: Keystone State

CAPITAL: Harrisburg

STATEHOOD: December 12, 1787 (2nd)

MOTTO: Virtue, liberty, and independence.

POPULATION: 12,287,150 (6th)

AREA: 46,058 sq. mi. (33rd)
(119,239 sq km)

HIGHEST POINT: 3,213 ft. (Mount Davis)

LOWEST POINT: Sea level (Delaware River)

FLOWER: Mountain laurel

TREE: Hemlock

BIRD: Ruffed grouse

FISH: Brook trout

Pennsylvania

Like neighboring West Virginia, Pennsylvania is a coal state. Its plentiful energy resources once fueled major steel factories in Pittsburgh, Allentown, and elsewhere. Now with most of those mills closed, the air is cleaner, but some local economies have yet to recover.

Easing that economic burden has been the state's robust food-processing industry. Pennsylvania leads the nation in the production of snack foods, especially potato chips, pretzels, and chocolate. It also ranks fourth in milk production and fourth in ice cream making.

Without all this agriculture, the cities of Philadelphia (the fifth largest in the nation by population) and Pittsburgh (the fifty-second largest by population) might otherwise dominate the state. Instead, the character of Pennsylvania has remained largely rural, with values and interests to match. The two most popular pastimes in western Pennsylvania, for example, are high school football and deer hunting.

Overall, mountains and rivers dominate the landscape, particularly atop the Appalachian Plateau covering northern and western Pennsylvania. In the southeastern corner of the state, across the Allegheny Mountains, a stretch of the Piedmont underlies the fertile farmland of Pennsylvania Dutch country. Beyond lies Philadelphia, perched on a tiny strip of the Atlantic Coastal Plain. Philadelphia and Erie, the state's two most important ports, give Pennsylvania access to both the Atlantic Ocean (via the Delaware River) and the Great Lakes.

Pennsylvania has more than a million licensed hunters of all ages. When its two-week buck-hunting season begins on the first Monday after Thanksgiving, cities across the state become ghost towns. Schools close and businesses run short of help as up to one third of a town's population heads for the woods.

During the nineteenth century, many Amish and Mennonite farmers settled in Lancaster County. Because they came from Germany (and not Holland), one might wonder why they're called the Pennsylvania Dutch. The reason is that the German word for "German" is *Deutsch,* which looks and sounds like *Dutch.*

Three Rivers
At Pittsburgh, once the nation's busiest inland port, the Allegheny and Monongahela rivers meet to form the Ohio. The Ohio River then flows southwest, joining the Mississippi at Cairo, Illinois.

Interstate
Highways

National
Parks and Refuges

Public Parks

Places of Interest

| 0 | miles | 2 |
| 0 | kilometers | 3.2 |

MARYLAND

Silver Spring

Bethesda

Chevy Chase

Rock Creek Park

Connecticut Ave.

Massachusetts Ave.

ROCK CREEK

Georgia Ave.

National Zoological Park

Rhode Island Ave.

National Arboretum

Although nearly half the people who live in D.C. work for Uncle Sam, the federal government isn't the only big industry in town. Tourists, from school groups to international visitors, fill up Washington's hotels and restaurants and provide jobs for ticket takers, museum curators, tour guides, and bus drivers.

The White House

Union Station

Anacostia River Park

Lincoln Memorial

Arlington

The Mall

U.S. Capitol

Fort DuPont Park

Arlington National Cemetery

Washington Monument

Jefferson Memorial

East Potomac Park

ANACOSTIA RIVER

VIRGINIA

The Pentagon

Washington National Airport

Bolling Air Force Base

POTOMAC RIVER

Alexandria

DID YOU KNOW?
that nearly one in ten D.C. residents is a lawyer?

11.5 miles (18.5 km)

ABOUT WASHINGTON, D.C.

NICKNAME: __

CAPITAL: __

STATEHOOD: __

MOTTO: Justice for all.

POPULATION: 571,822

AREA: 68 sq. mi.
(176 sq km)

HIGHEST POINT: 410 ft. (Tenleytown)

LOWEST POINT: 1 ft. (Potomac River)

FLOWER: American Beauty rose

TREE: Scarlet oak

BIRD: Wood thrush

Washington, D.C.

Each year, nearly twenty million people visit the District of Columbia. They come to see the White House, the Smithsonian Institution, and other popular tourist attractions. The grandeur of Washington's public architecture and the elegance of its street plan have led many to compare the city favorably with the most gracious European capitals. Yet when travelers arrive, they cannot help but find another Washington existing within the nation's capital, a troubled city in which poverty obscures all the wealth, privilege, and influence.

Until 1974, congressional committees governed the district. Then, in response to public pressure, Congress passed the Home Rule Act establishing a locally elected government. Sadly, this government functioned poorly. Crime rates rose, and streets became potholed, causing Congress to take back control of most city functions in 1995.

D.C. residents, two thirds of whom are black, have no voting representative in Congress because the district isn't part of any state. (The land was given to the federal government by Maryland in 1791.) However, D.C. residents do benefit greatly from the presence of the federal government, which provides hundreds of thousands of jobs and creates many other business opportunities. The presence of so many foreign embassies and international organizations also makes Washington a remarkably cosmopolitan place to live.

Originally, Washington was just one city within the District of Columbia. Today, it fills the entire district, and its metro area extends well beyond into the neighboring suburbs of Maryland and Virginia.

Many American cities suffer from urban problems such as crime and homelessness. In Washington, D.C., those problems have been particularly severe. For example, D.C. schools have a dropout rate close to 40 percent, the highest in the nation, and the poverty there can resemble that of an underdeveloped country.

When it was first surveyed in 1791, the District of Columbia formed a square ten miles (16 km) on each side, including land on both banks of the Potomac. In 1846, however, the federal government gave Virginia back its land, reducing the district's size from one hundred to sixty-eight square miles (259 to 176 sq km).

George Washington had the new federal city built at the head of navigation of the Potomac River— that is, at the point beyond which ships couldn't sail upstream because of rapids and waterfalls.

CANADA

POTOMAC RIVER

West
Virginia
page 60

Virginia
page 58

OHIO RIVER

Kentucky
page 46

ROANOKE RIVER

CUMBERLAND RIVER

North Carolina
page 52

Arkansas
page 40

Tennessee
page 56

TENNESSEE RIVER

South
Carolina
page 54

ARKANSAS RIVER

MISSISSIPPI RIVER

SAVANNAH RIVER

CHATTAHOOCHEE RIVER

RED RIVER

Alabama
page 38

Georgia
page 44

ATLANTIC OCEAN

SABINE RIVER

Louisiana
page 48

Mississippi
page 50

Florida
page 42

THE BAHAMAS

GULF OF MEXICO

CUBA

For geographical purposes, it sometimes makes sense to divide the southern states into three groups. Virginia, the Carolinas, Georgia, and Florida make up the seaboard states. With the exception of Florida, they all slope down from the Appalachian Mountains through the Piedmont to the Atlantic Coastal Plain. On the other hand, much of Alabama, Mississippi, Louisiana, and Arkansas is bottomland, enriched by the annual flooding of rivers such as the Mississippi. Finally, Tennessee, Kentucky, and West Virginia sit atop the rugged Appalachian highlands.

South

Rocket City, U.S.A.

In 1960, the National Aeronautics and Space Administration (NASA) opened the George C. Marshall Space Flight Center in Huntsville. Since then, many highly trained engineers from around the country have moved to Huntsville to work for the numerous rocketry companies now located there.

DID YOU KNOW?

that half of all U.S. peanuts are grown within one hundred miles (161 km) of Dothan, the self-styled Peanut Capital of the World?

TENNESSEE

Florence • • Wheeler Lake • Huntsville
TENNESSEE RIVER
565
• Tupelo
Decatur •
65
CUMBERLAND MTS.
Guntersville Lake
59
GEORGIA
• Gadsden
Weiss Lake
Lewis Smith Lake
Birmingham
Anniston •
• Atlanta
BLACK WARRIOR R.
• Hoover
20
459
COOSA RIVER
TALLAPOOSA RIVER
West Point Lake
• Tuscaloosa
Lake Martin
59 20
• Auburn
85
MISSISSIPPI
Selma •
65
Montgomery ✪
• Columbus
TOMBIGBEE RIVER
BLACK BELT
Tuskegee •
Phenix City
ALABAMA RIVER
• Troy
CHATTAHOOCHEE RIVER
Poorch Creek Reservation
CONECUH RIVER
65
• Andalusia
Dothan •
MOBILE RIVER
PERDIDO R.
Mobile •
10
10
• Pensacola
FLORIDA
Mobile Bay

GULF OF MEXICO

◄———————— 189 miles (304 km) ————————►

ABOUT ALABAMA

NICKNAME: Heart of Dixie
CAPITAL: Montgomery
STATEHOOD: December 14, 1819 (22nd)
MOTTO: We dare defend our rights.

POPULATION: 4,464,356 (23rd)
AREA: 52,423 sq. mi. (30th)
(135,717 sq km)
HIGHEST POINT: 2,405 ft. (Cheaha Mountain)
LOWEST POINT: Sea level (Gulf of Mexico)

FLOWER: Camellia
TREE: Southern pine
BIRD: Yellowhammer
FISH: Largemouth bass, tarpon

Alabama

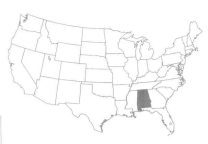

Which changed Alabama more: the Civil War or the boll weevil? Don't answer too quickly. Even after the Civil War, cotton farming continued to dominate the economy, while blacks still suffered from segregation and worse. Then, in 1915, an insect pest called the boll weevil infested Alabama's cotton fields. At the same time, the steel factories in Birmingham began to boom, offering jobs that lured many farm families from the countryside to the city. Together, the boll weevil and the steel jobs urbanized and industrialized what had been a thoroughly rural state.

Today in Alabama, steel, like cotton, has faded in importance, yet new manufacturing industries have taken its place. Paper mills, for example, thrive in Mobile and Montgomery, which makes sense for Alabama because forests cover two-thirds of the state. Culturally, though, many Alabamans prefer to revere the past, proudly maintaining many traditions commonly associated with the Old South. Some of these are positive, such as the leisurely pace of life, especially during the region's long, hot summers; others reflect problems that still need to be solved, such as the lingering poverty in the countryside.

Although it's difficult to tell from the ground, Alabama is tilted like a washboard. From the state's northeastern corner, where the Appalachian Mountains begin, the land slopes gradually down to the south and west. Following the land, most of Alabama's rivers flow southwest into Mobile Bay.

Traditions are important in Alabama, where most residents can trace their roots back to the nineteenth century. In the black community, which makes up one-fourth of the state, churches have been particularly active in social and political causes. Martin Luther King, Jr., for example, began his ministerial career at the Dexter Avenue Baptist Church in Montgomery (pictured above).

The key raw materials used in making iron and steel are iron ore, coal, and limestone. Alabama is the only place in the world where these three ingredients can be found within a ten-mile (sixteen-kilometer) radius.

Millions of years ago, the Gulf of Mexico covered southern Alabama. When it receded, it left behind a strip of rich, dark soil called the Black Belt. Once home to grand cotton plantations, the Black Belt now provides pastureland for cattle.

LEGEND

 Interstate Highways

 State Capital

National Parks and Refuges

 National Forests

▲ **Highest Point**

0	miles	50
0	kilometers	80

Even though Arkansas farmers produce nearly half of the nation's rice, the state's most important agricultural product is the broiler chicken. (Broilers are young chickens about seven weeks old.) Arkansas-based Tyson Foods, the world's largest poultry company, processes about forty million birds each week.

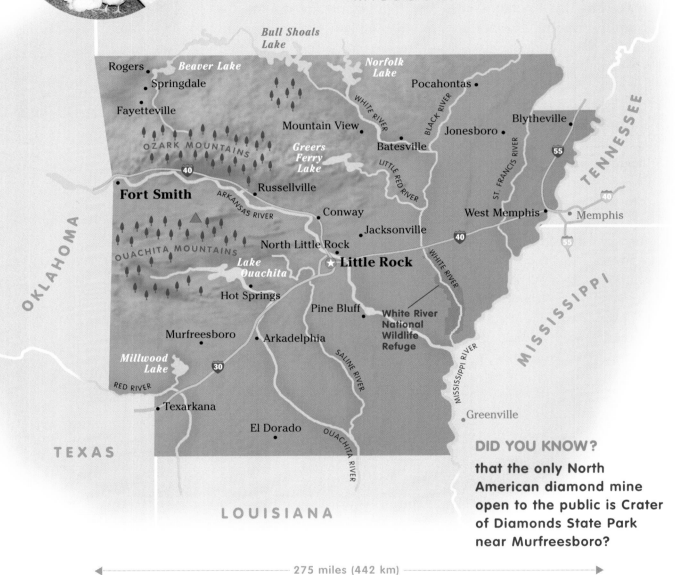

MISSOURI

Bull Shoals Lake

Rogers
Springdale
Fayetteville

Beaver Lake
Norfolk Lake

Pocahontas

WHITE RIVER
BLACK RIVER

Blytheville

Mountain View
Batesville
Jonesboro

OZARK MOUNTAINS
Greers Ferry Lake
LITTLE RED RIVER
ST. FRANCIS RIVER

55

Fort Smith
ARKANSAS RIVER
Russellville
Conway
West Memphis
Memphis

OUACHITA MOUNTAINS
Jacksonville

40

40

North Little Rock
★ **Little Rock**
WHITE RIVER

55

Lake Ouachita
Hot Springs
Pine Bluff
White River National Wildlife Refuge

Murfreesboro
Arkadelphia

SALINE RIVER

Millwood Lake
RED RIVER

30

MISSISSIPPI RIVER

MISSISSIPPI

Texarkana

El Dorado
OUACHITA RIVER

Greenville

TEXAS

OKLAHOMA

TENNESSEE

LOUISIANA

DID YOU KNOW?

that the only North American diamond mine open to the public is Crater of Diamonds State Park near Murfreesboro?

◄———————— 275 miles (442 km) ————————►

ABOUT ARKANSAS

NICKNAME: Natural State
CAPITAL: Little Rock
STATEHOOD: June 15, 1836 (25th)
MOTTO: The people rule.

POPULATION: 2,692,090 (33rd)
AREA: 53,182 sq. mi. (29th)
(137,682 sq km)
HIGHEST POINT: 2,753 ft. (Magazine Mt.)
LOWEST POINT: 55 ft. (Ouachita River)

FLOWER: Apple blossom
TREE: Pine
BIRD: Mockingbird

Arkansas

Little Rock, the state capital, is more than Arkansas's economic and political hub: It's very nearly the wheel itself. Outside this modern city, the rest of the state is mostly countryside. In many towns, people live so far apart that there is no Main Street or downtown shopping area. Although tourism has brought many visitors to Arkansas in recent years, the people who live there have changed remarkably little. Nearly 99 percent of them were born in the United States, and more than two thirds were born in Arkansas itself. As a result, the state's population, though racially mixed, isn't culturally diverse.

A diagonal line drawn across Arkansas from the northeast to the southwest would separate the state's lowlands from its highlands. Above this line, which would pass through Little Rock, would be two mountain ranges: the Ouachitas and the Ozarks. The Ouachitas are known for their hot springs, which Native Americans visited for thousands of years before white settlers arrived. The isolated Ozark Plateau features broad ridges and deep valleys cut by fast-moving streams. Separating these ranges is the Arkansas River Valley. Like nearly every river in the state, the Arkansas flows southeast and empties into the Mississippi.

Pine forests cover much of the Arkansas lowlands, yet near the Mississippi River the land has been cleared to allow farming. Once the warm, moist soil produced large harvests of cotton. Now soybeans and rice are the most profitable crops.

During the 1960s, when new roads were built in the Ozarks to encourage tourism, the region became less isolated but also lost some of its individuality. Now the Ozark Folk Center in Mountain View preserves many fading traditions of the mountain people, including their music and crafts such as wood carving and quilt making.

143°F

How Hot Are the Hot Springs?

Two million people a year visit the resort town of Hot Springs on the eastern edge of the Ouachita Mountains. Most go to bathe in the naturally hot mineral water that bubbles from the ground there at 143°F (62°C). According to local Native American tradition, this water is warmed by the breath of the Great Spirit.

The dense pine and hardwood forests that cover the Ozark Plateau once made travel difficult. In this way, the terrain contributed to the isolation of the people who lived there.

LEGEND

- **Interstate Highways**
- **State Capital**
- **National Parks and Refuges**
- **Marshlands**
- **Highest Point**

0 miles 50
0 kilometers 80

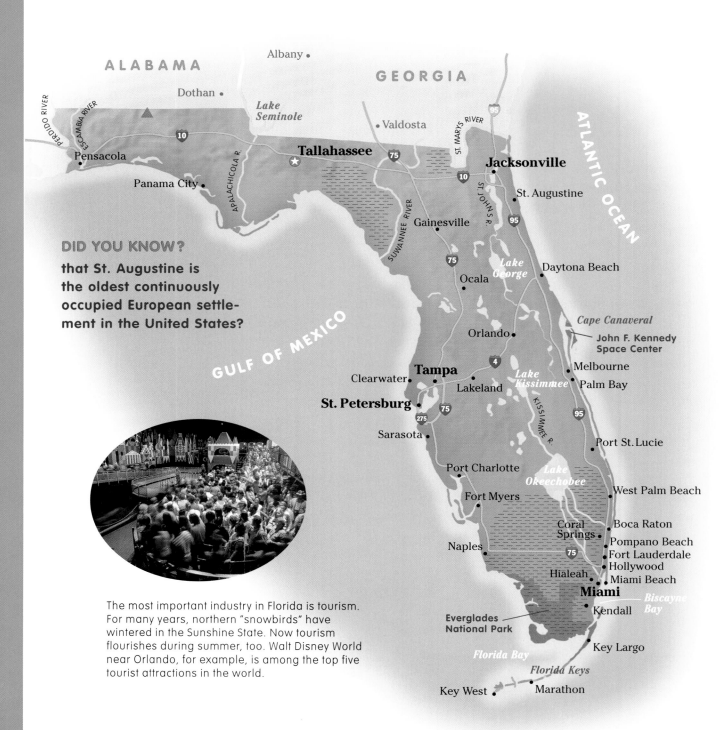

ALABAMA

GEORGIA

Albany

Dothan

Lake Seminole

Valdosta

PERDIDO RIVER

ESCAMBIA RIVER

Pensacola

Panama City

APALACHICOLA R.

Tallahassee

ST. MARYS RIVER

Jacksonville

St. Augustine

ATLANTIC OCEAN

SUWANNEE RIVER

Gainesville

ST. JOHNS R.

DID YOU KNOW?

that St. Augustine is the oldest continuously occupied European settlement in the United States?

Lake George

Ocala

Daytona Beach

Cape Canaveral

John F. Kennedy Space Center

GULF OF MEXICO

Orlando

Clearwater

Tampa

Lakeland

Lake Kissimmee

Melbourne

Palm Bay

KISSIMMEE R.

St. Petersburg

Sarasota

Port Charlotte

Fort Myers

Port St. Lucie

Lake Okeechobee

West Palm Beach

Naples

Coral Springs

Boca Raton

Pompano Beach

Fort Lauderdale

Hollywood

Hialeah

Miami Beach

Miami

Kendall

Biscayne Bay

Everglades National Park

Florida Bay

Key Largo

Florida Keys

Key West

Marathon

The most important industry in Florida is tourism. For many years, northern "snowbirds" have wintered in the Sunshine State. Now tourism flourishes during summer, too. Walt Disney World near Orlando, for example, is among the top five tourist attractions in the world.

← 361 miles (581 km) →

ABOUT FLORIDA

NICKNAME: Sunshine State
CAPITAL: Tallahassee
STATEHOOD: March 3, 1845 (27th)
MOTTO: In God we trust.

POPULATION: 16,396,515 (4th)
AREA: 65,756 sq. mi. (22nd)
(170,234 sq km)
HIGHEST POINT: 345 ft. (Walton County)
LOWEST POINT: Sea level (Atlantic Ocean)

FLOWER: Orange blossom
TREE: Sabal palm
BIRD: Mockingbird

Florida

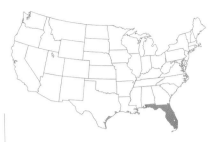

The typically warm, sunny weather in Florida affects nearly every aspect of life there. Nearly seventy million tourists a year visit the state to enjoy its tropical climate, and the plentiful sunshine also attracts many retirees. In fact, so many older Americans have moved to Florida, the southernmost of the continental states, that it now has the highest percentage of residents over age sixty-five of any state. Another factor contributing to the diversity of Florida's population is immigration, particularly the arrival of many Cuban and Haitian refugees. Overall, Florida has one of the lowest percentages of residents who were born in the state.

Many of the newcomers, especially the well-to-do retirees, live in condominiums lining the bone-white Gold Coast beaches between Miami and West Palm Beach. The Florida Keys, small limestone-and-coral islands off the state's southern tip, are another chic resort area. Northern Florida, however, is predominantly rural, resembling its neighbors Alabama and Georgia much more than it resembles urban, Latin-flavored Miami.

Finally, Florida is the flattest state. Its highest point, in the Panhandle near the Alabama border, is 345 feet (105 m) above sea level. Farther south, on the peninsula separating the Atlantic Ocean from the Gulf of Mexico, the average elevation is less than 100 feet (30 m) above sea level.

Florida's Spanish Accent

In 1513, Spanish explorer Juan Ponce de León became the first European to discover Florida. Since then, Hispanic culture has been an important part of Florida's architecture, cuisine, and lifestyle. Today, most Spanish-speaking Floridians live in and around Miami, where many Cubans have settled.

The orchards of central Florida dominate U.S. citrus production. About 80 percent of the nation's oranges and grapefruit are grown in the state, where nine out of every ten oranges are used to make orange juice.

Florida's most unusual topographical feature, and one of the country's most important wildlife refuges, is the Everglades. Although most people think of the Everglades as a swamp, it's actually a shallow river fifty miles (80 km) wide that carries overflow from Lake Okeechobee into Florida Bay. Its average depth is six inches (15 cm).

LEGEND

Interstate Highways

State Capital

■ **National Parks and Refuges**

National Forests

Marshlands

▲ **Highest Point**

0	miles	50
0	kilometers	80

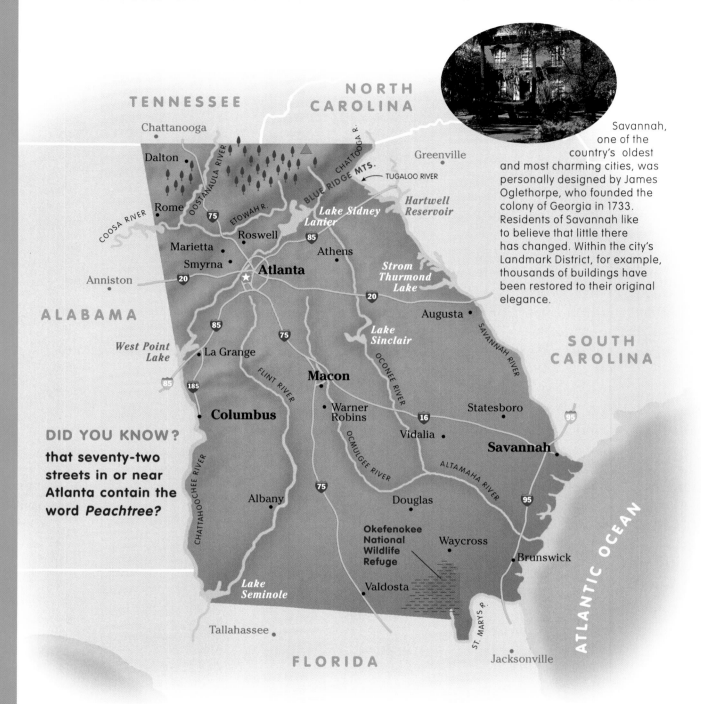

TENNESSEE

NORTH CAROLINA

Chattanooga

Dalton

OOSTANAULA RIVER

Rome

COOSA RIVER

ETOWAH R.

75

Roswell

Marietta

Smyrna

Anniston

20

ALABAMA

West Point Lake

85

La Grange

FLINT RIVER

185

Columbus

CHATTAHOOCHEE RIVER

Albany

Lake Seminole

Tallahassee

FLORIDA

BLUE RIDGE MTS.

CHATTOOGA R.

TUGALOO RIVER

Greenville

Hartwell Reservoir

Lake Sidney Lanier

85

Athens

★ **Atlanta**

Strom Thurmond Lake

20

Augusta

SAVANNAH RIVER

SOUTH CAROLINA

Lake Sinclair

OCONEE RIVER

Macon

75

Warner Robins

16

Statesboro

95

Vidalia

OCMULGEE RIVER

Savannah

ALTAMAHA RIVER

75

Douglas

95

Okefenokee National Wildlife Refuge

Waycross

Valdosta

Brunswick

ST. MARYS R.

Jacksonville

ATLANTIC OCEAN

DID YOU KNOW?

that seventy-two streets in or near Atlanta contain the word *Peachtree*?

Savannah, one of the country's oldest and most charming cities, was personally designed by James Oglethorpe, who founded the colony of Georgia in 1733. Residents of Savannah like to believe that little there has changed. Within the city's Landmark District, for example, thousands of buildings have been restored to their original elegance.

← 254 miles (409 km) →

ABOUT GEORGIA

NICKNAME: Empire State of the South
CAPITAL: Atlanta
STATEHOOD: January 2, 1788 (4th)
MOTTO: Wisdom, justice, moderation.

POPULATION: 8,383,915 (10th)
AREA: 59,441 sq. mi. (24th)
(153,886 sq km)
HIGHEST POINT: 4,784 ft. (Brasstown Bald)
LOWEST POINT: Sea level (Atlantic Ocean)

FLOWER: Cherokee rose
TREE: Live oak
BIRD: Brown thrasher
FISH: Largemouth bass

Georgia

At one time a cotton state like its neighbors, Georgia now finds itself at the head of the New South, the name given to those states in the region that have successfully updated their economies. The key has been diversification. Today, cotton makes up just 8 percent of Georgia's farm income, with peanuts, pecans, and peaches gaining in importance. (Georgia now leads the nation in all three of these crops). The state also ranks high in the production of granite, marble, wood pulp, aircraft, textiles, and the fine china clays used to make dinnerware.

Another important step in Georgia's economic revival was the civil rights movement of the 1960s, which pushed the state to become more progressive and cosmopolitan. White Georgians learned to work with, not against, blacks, who make up more than one quarter of the population. Some black Georgians still live on farms, yet many more have moved to the cities, particularly Atlanta, where a strong black middle class has emerged.

In northern Georgia, the Blue Ridge Mountains dot the landscape with "balds," or treeless hilltops. From Atlanta southward, however, the belly of the state sits on the rolling Piedmont Plateau, which itself slopes down to the wetlands of the Atlantic and Gulf coastal plains. Along the Florida border is the huge Okefenokee Swamp, one of the nation's leading bird refuges. In the language of the Seminole, *okefenokee* means "land of the trembling earth."

Any item of woven or knit cloth is generally called a textile. Although Georgia trails North Carolina in overall textile production, it leads the nation in carpet making. The center of this industry is the Dalton area, which produces 80 percent of the nation's carpeting.

Atlanta, the acknowledged capital of the New South, has been sucking up Georgians like a vacuum cleaner. At least two out of every five now live within the Atlanta metropolitan area, which has become the most important commercial, financial, and transportation center south of Washington, D.C., and east of Dallas.

Georgia's Piedmont Plateau is known for its red clay hills. "I have a dream," Atlanta native Martin Luther King, Jr., said in his famous speech, "that one day on the red hills of Georgia, sons of former slaves and the sons of former slave owners will be able to sit down together at the table of brotherhood."

LEGEND

20 Interstate Highways   ✪ State Capital   ■ National Parks and Refuges   🌲 National Forests   ▲ Highest Point

0 — miles — 50
0 — kilometers — 80

Most Kentucky coal is strip-mined by power shovels that tear away the surface layer of trees, rocks, and soil. Because strip mining can pollute streams and destroy animal habitats, Kentuckians often have to choose between a healthy economy and a healthy ecology.

DID YOU KNOW ?

that bluegrass gets its name from the tiny bluish blossoms that the green grass produces each May?

350 miles (563 km)

ABOUT KENTUCKY

NICKNAME: Bluegrass State	**POPULATION:** 4,065,556 (25th)	**FLOWER:** Goldenrod
CAPITAL: Frankfort	**AREA:** 40,411 sq. mi. (37th)	**TREE:** Tulip tree
STATEHOOD: June 1, 1792 (15th)	(104,619 sq km)	**BIRD:** Kentucky cardinal
MOTTO: United we stand, divided we fall.	**HIGHEST POINT:** 4,139 ft. (Black Mountain)	**FISH:** Bass
	LOWEST POINT: 257 ft. (Mississippi River)	

Kentucky

More so than other states, Kentucky is both rich and poor, beautiful and ugly. Its many waterways are among the most scenic in the nation, but elsewhere strip mining for coal has scarred the landscape. Similarly, great wealth exists alongside enduring poverty. In the Cumberland coalfields, labor unions have struggled for decades, sometimes violently, to raise unfairly low wages and improve dangerous working conditions. Yet not too far away, Lexington's immaculate horse farms recall the splendor and gentility of the pre–Civil War South.

Although the Kentucky economy has diversified in recent years—adding automobile plants, for example—it continues to depend on two traditional exports: coal and tobacco. Kentucky ranks second in tobacco behind North Carolina and third in coal behind Wyoming and West Virginia. Other notable Kentucky products are bourbon whiskey and grass seed.

Six major geographical regions cover the state: The coal-rich Cumberland Plateau, part of the Appalachian chain, dominates eastern Kentucky. In the north, surrounding Lexington, are the rolling fields of the Bluegrass. Enclosing the Bluegrass is a horseshoe-shaped line of hills called the Knobs, to the south and west of which lies the flat fertile Pennyroyal. Along the Ohio River are the Western Coal Fields, while in the southwestern corner is the Jackson Purchase, an area bounded by the Mississippi, Tennessee, and Ohio rivers and named after Andrew Jackson, who helped buy it from the Chickasaw in 1818.

Bluegrass, the folk music of this predominantly rural state, resembles old-time string-band music, except that it's faster, higher pitched, and more strident. Bill Monroe, who grew up in Rosine, developed the bluegrass style after World War II. Bluegrass features mandolins, fiddles, and especially banjos.

Beneath the Pennyroyal near Bowling Green is Mammoth Cave, the largest known cave system in the world. Its maze of tunnels and chambers was formed over millions of years by water trickling through limestone bedrock. So far, explorers have charted more than 350 miles (560 km) of tunnels on five underground levels.

The Bluegrass region provides nearly ideal conditions for raising thoroughbred racehorses. The lush grass on which these horses feed absorbs calcium from the limestone bedrock. This calcium promotes strong bones and muscles. The best thoroughbreds compete each May in the Kentucky Derby, run at the Churchill Downs racetrack in Louisville.

LEGEND

 Interstate Highways   State Capital   ■ National Parks and Refuges   National Forests   Marshlands   ▲ Highest Point

| 0 | miles | 50 |
| 0 | kilometers | 80 |

Texarkana

ARKANSAS

Caddo Lake

Lake Claiborne

Lake Bayou D'Arbonne

Shreveport

20

Bossier City

20

Monroe

OUACHITA RIVER

Vicksburg

RED RIVER

TENSAS RIVER

MISSISSIPPI

Catahoula Lake

Toledo Bend Reservoir

Alexandria

BLACK R.

Natchez

TEXAS

De Ridder

49

ATCHAFALAYA R.

MISSISSIPPI RIVER

55

Baton Rouge

10

12

12

Slidell

59

PEARL RIVER

Lake Maurepas

55

10

Lake Pontchartrain

Kenner

10

Beaumont

Lake Charles

10

Lafayette

Metairie

New Orleans

Sabine National Wildlife Refuge

SABINE RIVER

Grand Lake

New Iberia

Six Mile Lake

Calcasieu Lake

White Lake

Houma

MISSISSIPPI RIVER

DID YOU KNOW?

that because the early French and Spanish rulers of Louisiana were all Catholics, the state is divided into parishes rather than counties?

GULF OF MEXICO

Offshore oil and gas exploration was pioneered off the coast of Louisiana. The state is currently the nation's fourth leading petroleum producer (behind Texas, Alaska, and California) and its second leading producer of natural gas (behind Texas).

◄———————— 237 miles (381 km) ————————►

ABOUT LOUISIANA

NICKNAME: Pelican State
CAPITAL: Baton Rouge
STATEHOOD: April 30, 1812 (18th)
MOTTO: Union, justice, confidence.

POPULATION: 4,465,430 (22nd)
AREA: 51,843 sq. mi. (31st)
(134,215 sq km)
HIGHEST POINT: 535 ft. (Driskill Mountain)
LOWEST POINT: -8 ft. (New Orleans)

FLOWER: Magnolia
TREE: Bald cypress
BIRD: Brown pelican

South • Louisiana

48

Louisiana

Before the United States purchased Louisiana in 1803, it had been both a French and a Spanish colony. There were also slaves in the territory, brought to work on the numerous cotton plantations. Over time, these three cultures merged to form what is today known as Creole.

The Cajuns, who live in Louisiana's southern bayous, also have French roots, yet they came to Louisiana by way of Canada. In 1755, the British expelled about ten thousand French colonists from Acadia (now Nova Scotia), and many made their way south to Louisiana. Lately, the national popularity of zydeco music has stimulated a resurgence of the Cajun French language and culture.

Blacks, who make up 32 percent of the population, were long denied economic and political power in Louisiana. Yet they made important cultural contributions. Jazz music, for example, was invented by black performers in New Orleans about 1900.

Although agriculture remains important in Louisiana, the state's economy now depends more on shipping, petroleum, and the chemical industry. Between Baton Rouge and New Orleans, the banks of the Mississippi River are lined with chemical plants and oil refineries. In general, the Mississippi dominates the physical geography of the state. The southern half of Louisiana is remarkably flat, with low-lying swamps and a beachless coastline. As one moves north, however, the land rises slowly to prairies and low hills.

Nothing shows off Louisiana's rich cultural mix so much as its cooking. The world-famous Creole cuisine of New Orleans is a distinctive yet elegant blend of French, Spanish, and African dishes. In bayou country, however, Cajuns favor much spicier food, such as gumbo (a stew) and jambalaya (a rice dish).

Rivers are constantly depositing sediment along their banks as well as on their bottoms. Sometimes this sediment builds up so high that the river rises to a level above that of the surrounding land. This has happened at New Orleans, where levees have been constructed to protect the city from flooding.

A bayou is a stream that moves slowly through marshland. The bayous of southern Louisiana provide important habitats for migrating birds, especially the wild ducks and geese that winter there.

49

LEGEND

🛡20 Interstate Highways	✪ State Capital	⬜ Native American Reservations	🌲 National Forests	⬛ National Parks and Refuges	▲ Highest Point	0 miles 50		
						0 kilometers 80		

TENNESSEE

Memphis

Pickwick Lake

Southaven

Holly Springs

Sardis Lake

TENNESSEE HILLS ▲

ARKANSAS

Oxford

Tupelo

Clarksdale

🛡55

YALOBUSHA R.

TOMBIGBEE RIVER

Cleveland

Grenada Lake

Columbus

TALLAHATCHIE R.

Greenwood

Starkville

Greenville

YAZOO RIVER

BLACK PRAIRIE

Yazoo City

Mississippi Choctaw Reservation

ALABAMA

BIG BLACK RIVER

Ross Barnett Reservoir

🛡20

Vicksburg

★ Jackson

🛡20 🛡59

Meridian

MISSISSIPPI RIVER

LOUISIANA

PEARL RIVER

Laurel

Natchez

🛡55

Hattiesburg

Mississippi Sandhill Crane National Wildlife Refuge

🛡59

Mobile

DID YOU KNOW?

that Mississippi Delta topsoil can be as deep as twenty-five feet (8 m) in some places?

Baton Rouge

Gulfport

🛡10

Biloxi

Pascagoula

New Orleans

GULF OF MEXICO

In Mississippi, many farmers have turned unproductive cotton fields into profitable catfish farms by flooding them. These aquaculturists fatten young catfish on grain before harvesting them, just as any farmer would fatten a cow or chicken before sending it to the slaughterhouse.

◄········ 188 miles (302 km) ········►

ABOUT MISSISSIPPI

NICKNAME: Magnolia State

CAPITAL: Jackson

STATEHOOD: December 10, 1817 (20th)

MOTTO: By valor and arms.

POPULATION: 2,858,029 (31st)

AREA: 48,434 sq. mi. (32nd) (125,390 sq km)

HIGHEST POINT: 806 ft. (Woodall Mountain)

LOWEST POINT: Sea level (Gulf of Mexico)

FLOWER: Magnolia

TREE: Magnolia

BIRD: Mockingbird

FISH: Largemouth bass

Mississippi

Of all the states in the Union, Mississippi had the hardest time transitioning from the nineteenth century. The core of the problem was the poor relationship between whites and blacks. (Blacks in Mississippi make up 36 percent of the population, the highest percentage of any state.) The hostility that existed between these two groups from the Civil War until the 1960s virtually guaranteed that Mississippi would place last year after year in nearly every economic ranking. Yet the remarkable courage and wisdom shown by black Mississippians during the civil rights movement taught a majority of whites that keeping blacks down meant keeping Mississippi down as well. Since the 1970s, whites and blacks have worked together, and conditions in Mississippi have greatly improved.

Agriculture remains fundamental to the economy of this mainly rural state, yet manufacturing has become an increasingly vital part of the mix. In recent years, for example, many Mississippians have moved south to work in the shipyards at Pascagoula or for one of the oil and gas companies lining the Gulf Coast.

Although not as important economically as it once was, the Mississippi River remains the most important geographic feature in the state's flat landscape. The river's floodplain, a region known as the Delta, is quite narrow south of Vicksburg. In northern Mississippi, however, it widens to include the entire basin between the Mississippi and Yazoo rivers.

Faulkner Country
Mississippi has produced many great writers, including Eudora Welty, Tennessee Williams, and especially William Faulkner. Setting his books in small-town Mississippi, Faulkner made fictional Yoknapatawpha County one of the most celebrated locations in American literature. For the last thirty years of his life, Faulkner lived at Rowan Oak in Oxford (pictured above).

Most naturally occurring lakes in Mississippi are oxbows, formed by sudden changes in the course of the Mississippi River. Although the center of the river marks the state's boundary with Louisiana and Arkansas, land cut off from Mississippi by abrupt course changes still belongs to Mississippi.

The topsoil of the Mississippi Delta is particularly rich because for thousands of years annual flooding dumped tons and tons of silt over the land. Now artificial levees of earth, sand, rock, and concrete keep the river generally within its banks.

LEGEND

[20] Interstate Highways ⊛ State Capital ▦ Native American Reservations 🌲 National Forests ■ National Parks and Refuges ▨ Marshlands ▲ Highest Point

0 miles 50
0 km 80

North Carolina leads the nation in the production of both tobacco and tobacco products, such as cigarettes. Tobacco fields blanket much of the Piedmont, where farmers have been reluctant to give up their way of life (and suffer financial hardship) even though tobacco has been shown to be a health hazard.

VIRGINIA

Buggs Island Lake

Virginia Beach

TENN.

Great Smoky Mountains National Park

YADKIN RIVER

[77]

Greensboro Burlington

Lake Gaston

[85]

ROANOKE R.

CHOWAN R.

Winston-Salem

Durham

[95]

BLUE RIDGE MOUNTAINS

Knoxville

CATAWBA R.

High Point

Chapel Hill

Raleigh ★ Rocky Mount

Asheville

[40]

Lake Norman

[85]

UHARIE R.

Cary

[40]

Wilson

Greenville

[26]

Cherokee Reservation

Gastonia

Lake Tillery

Goldsboro

NEUSE RIVER

Cape Hatteras

[85]

Charlotte

PEE DEE RIVER

Fayetteville

[40]

[77]

[95]

CAPE FEAR RIVER

Jacksonville

Cape Lookout

SOUTH CAROLINA

Wilmington

GEORGIA

Columbia

Cape Fear

ATLANTIC OCEAN

DID YOU KNOW?

that North Carolina's Mount Mitchell is the highest point east of the Mississippi River?

503 miles (809 km)

ABOUT NORTH CAROLINA

NICKNAME: Tar Heel State
CAPITAL: Raleigh
STATEHOOD: November 21, 1789 (12th)
MOTTO: To be rather than to seem.

POPULATION: 8,186,268 (11th)
AREA: 53,821 sq. mi. (28th)
(139,336 sq km)
HIGHEST POINT: 6,684 ft. (Mount Mitchell)
LOWEST POINT: Sea level (Atlantic Ocean)

FLOWER: Flowering dogwood
TREE: Longleaf pine
BIRD: Cardinal
FISH: Channel bass

North Carolina

Most of North Carolina's major rivers begin along the state's western edge, where the Blue Ridge and Great Smoky mountains rise up to form the highest peaks in the long Appalachian chain. From these mountains, where the people practice handicrafts much as their ancestors did, the water flows east in narrow, swift-moving streams down to the Piedmont Plateau. That's where North Carolina's largest cities are located and where most of its money is made. On the busy Piedmont, furniture and textile manufacturers add considerably to the even larger profits of the tobacco industry.

Passing into the Tidewater region, North Carolina's rivers slow and widen as they spread across the Atlantic Coastal Plain. The pace of life in this rural area slows considerably as well. Extending about one hundred miles (161 km) inland, the Tidewater covers a great deal of marshland as well as the southern end of the Great Dismal Swamp. Because of their shallow estuaries, North Carolina's rivers don't make useful points of entry for shipping. However, the abundance of shrimp, blue crab, and flounder in the state's coastal waters makes them excellent for commercial fishing.

Overall, North Carolina ranks among the top ten states in industrial jobs. Yet wages remain low because so many of those jobs, especially in the tobacco industry, require little skill or training.

The thirteen thousand Cherokee in North Carolina make up one of the largest Native American populations east of the Mississippi River. Their reservation is located at the base of the Great Smoky Mountains, where their ancestors fled during the late 1830s to escape forced removal by the government.

Since 1959, local business leaders have been working with the three Triangle universities—Duke (in Durham), North Carolina State (in Raleigh), and the University of North Carolina at Chapel Hill—to create a world-class research facility. The result, Research Triangle Park, specializes in such high-tech fields as supercomputing and biotechnology.

The long, thin islands that fringe much of North Carolina's coast are called the Outer Banks. These enormous sandbars protect the mainland from high winds and erosion caused by the pounding Atlantic surf.

LEGEND

 Interstate Highways

 State Capital

National Parks and Refuges

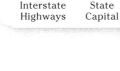 National Forests

Marshlands

▲ Highest Point

| 0 | miles | 50 |
| 0 | kilometers | 80 |

NORTH CAROLINA

Charlotte

BLUE RIDGE MOUNTAINS

CHATTOOGA R.

TUGALOO R.

Lake Keowee

SENECA R.

Greenville

Spartanburg

Wylie Lake

Rock Hill

CATAWBA RIVER

Cheraw

Hartwell Reservoir

Anderson

SALUDA RIVER

Wateree Lake

Florence

95

Greenwood

BROAD RIVER

Lake Murray

Columbia

CONGAREE R.

WATEREE R.

Sumter

95

Lake City

Strom Thurmond Lake

Augusta

Congaree Swamp National Monument

Orangeburg

Lake Marion

PEE DEE RIVER

Myrtle Beach

SANTEE RIVER

Georgetown

GEORGIA

SAVANNAH RIVER

Lake Moultrie

COOPER R.

Walterboro

Charleston

95

ATLANTIC OCEAN

Beaufort

Kiawah Island

Savannah

Hilton Head Island

DID YOU KNOW?
that South Carolina's coastal swamps are home to most of the poisonous snakes found in the United States?

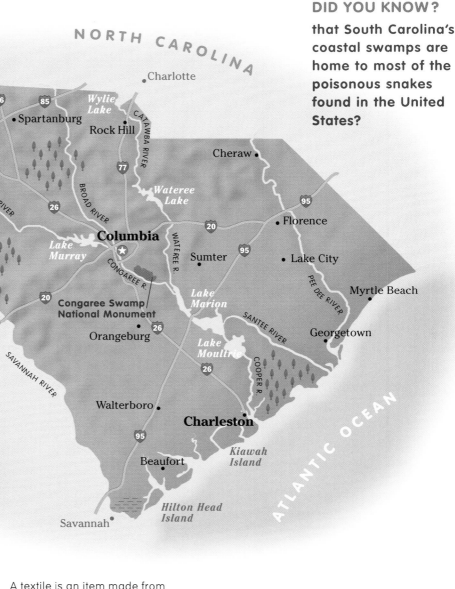

A textile is an item made from woven or knitted cloth. In South Carolina's Textile Belt, which runs through Spartanburg and Greenville, owners of textile factories benefit from a relatively low cost of labor.

◄----------------- 273 miles (439 km) -----------------►

ABOUT SOUTH CAROLINA

NICKNAME: Palmetto State

CAPITAL: Columbia

STATEHOOD: May 23, 1788 (8th)

MOTTO: While I breathe, I hope.

POPULATION: 4,063,011 (26th)

AREA: 32,008 sq. mi. (40th)
(82,865 sq km)

HIGHEST POINT: 3,560 ft. (Sassafras Mt.)

LOWEST POINT: Sea level (Atlantic Ocean)

FLOWER: Yellow jessamine

TREE: Palmetto

BIRD: Carolina wren

FISH: Striped bass

South Carolina

South Carolina, like its neighbors, was once an agricultural state dependent on cotton and slave labor. Since the Civil War, however, tobacco and greenhouse plants have overtaken cotton as the most important crops, just as other sectors of the economy have overtaken agriculture. Yet South Carolina retains much of its pre–Civil War cultural heritage. For example, the state's tradition of soldiering has been preserved at both The Citadel in Charleston, one of the nation's premier military colleges, and the renowned Marine Corps training center on Parris Island, near Beaufort.

When it comes to geography, the people of South Carolina like to keep things simple: They call the flat land near the coast the Low Country and everything else the Up Country. Covering about two thirds of the state, the Low Country—what geographers call the Atlantic Coastal Plain—features many slow-moving rivers that feed swamps and marshes near the coast.

The Up Country—or, more formally, the Piedmont Plateau—begins just west of Columbia, the state capital. Rising gradually from east to west, the Piedmont ends at the Blue Ridge Mountains, which cut across the northwestern corner of the state. Columbia itself sits atop a line of sandy hills marking the point at which the South Carolina shoreline once stood millions of years ago.

Many black descendants of slaves live on the Sea Islands, extending south into Georgia and Florida. Isolation has helped preserve their unique language, Gullah, which mixes seventeenth-century English with several African languages. *Goober* (meaning "peanut") and *hoodoo* (meaning "bad luck") were both originally Gullah words.

Los Angeles | 3,000 miles | New York

It's a Stretch

As the crow flies, South Carolina's coastline is 187 miles (301 km) long. However, because there are so many inlets and islands south of Georgetown, the coastline that you would walk along is actually much longer. If you could pull it straight, it would be about 3,000 miles (about 5,000 km) long—approximately the distance from Los Angeles to New York City.

From Pawleys Island (near Georgetown) to the North Carolina border stretches a sixty-mile (hundred-kilometer) crescent of white-sand beach called the Grand Strand. First among Grand Strand resorts is Myrtle Beach, a top-ten U.S. tourist destination.

Interstate Highways State Capital National Parks and Refuges National Forests Highest Point

| 0 | miles | 50 |
| 0 | kilometers | 80 |

During World War II, the War Department built in a hidden Cumberland Mountain valley a top-secret town for scientists working on the atom bomb. Today, researchers at the Oak Ridge National Laboratory conduct all sorts of experiments, such as this one to help detect airborne pollutants.

KENTUCKY

Cairo

Bowling Green

Kentucky Lake

MO.

VA.

Clarksville

Dale Hollow Lake

Union City

Paris

Reelfoot Lake

Cookeville

Norris Lake

Kingsport

Nashville

CUMBERLAND RIVER

CLINCH RIVER

Johnson City

ARK.

Humboldt

Center Hill Lake

Oak Ridge

Knoxville

Jackson

Murfreesboro

Columbia

Asheville

Shelbyville

Athens

N.C.

Memphis

Savannah

Tims Ford Lake

Cleveland

Great Smoky Mountains National Park

Fayetteville

Chattanooga

Pickwick Lake

Huntsville

S.C.

MISS.

GEORGIA

Tupelo

ALABAMA

•Atlanta

An aerial view of Oak Ridge National Laboratory.

DID YOU KNOW?

that Tennessee's only large natural lake, Reelfoot, was created when violent earthquakes in 1811 and 1812 formed a depression into which water from the Mississippi River flowed?

430 miles (692 km)

ABOUT TENNESSEE

NICKNAME: Volunteer State
CAPITAL: Nashville
STATEHOOD: June 1, 1796 (16th)
MOTTO: Agriculture and commerce.

POPULATION: 5,740,021 (16th)
AREA: 42,146 sq. mi. (36th)
(109,111 sq km)
HIGHEST POINT: 6,643 ft. (Clingmans Dome)
LOWEST POINT: 178 ft. (Mississippi River)

FLOWER: Iris
TREE: Tulip tree
BIRD: Mockingbird

Tennessee

Tennessee has always been a divided state. During the Civil War, for example, the mountain people of eastern Tennessee remained loyal to the Union while the residents of middle and western Tennessee seceded to join the Confederacy. As a result, more Civil War battles were fought in Tennessee than in any other state except Virginia.

In many ways, Tennessee remains a divided state, caught between North and South. Its culture, especially in western Tennessee, is profoundly southern in style and taste. Tennessee's economy, however, is much more northern in character. Because 70 percent of the state's land is considered unfit for cultivation, Tennessee has industrialized more rapidly than its neighbors. Until recently, the chemical industry was ranked first in the state, but now, with new automobile factories in Spring Hill (Saturn) and Smyrna (Nissan), transportation equipment tops the list of its products.

Rugged eastern Tennessee takes in both the Great Smoky Mountains and the high, hilly Cumberland Plateau. West of the Cumberland Mountains sits the Nashville Basin, the most prominent geographical feature of middle Tennessee, which ends at the Tennessee River. The flatlands on the other side of that river make up western Tennessee, whose principal city is Memphis. In addition to being the second largest inland port on the Mississippi, Memphis is the birthplace of rock'n'roll music. From 1948, the city was home to Elvis Presley, whose Graceland mansion still receives 650,000 visitors a year.

Nashville, the Tennessee state capital, is probably better known as the Country Music Capital of the World. Ever since radio station WSM began broadcasting live performances from the Grand Ole Opry in 1925, songwriters and performers have flocked to Nashville's Music Row to make it in the music business.

) dams

A Powerful River

In 1933, Congress created the Tennessee Valley Authority (TVA). Its mission was to build dams along the Tennessee River that would control flooding, improve navigation, and generate electricity. The TVA currently operates twenty-nine dams producing cheap hydroelectric power.

The Great Smoky Mountains of eastern Tennessee get their name from the bluish haze that usually covers them. This "smoke" is actually a mixture of water vapor and evaporated plant oils.

57

Interstate Highways

 State Capital

National Parks and Refuges

Marshlands

▲ Highest Point

0	miles	50
0	kilometers	80

The hub of the navy's Atlantic fleet is Hampton Roads, the deepwater channel through which the James River flows into Chesapeake Bay. Norfolk, site of the world's largest naval base, serves as home port to sixty-six ships, while Newport News Shipbuilding, the largest privately owned U.S. shipyard, builds everything from tugboats to nuclear-powered aircraft carriers.

MARYLAND

Winchester

Baltimore

Shenandoah National Park

81

Arlington

Washington, D.C.

66

Alexandria

WEST VIRGINIA

Harrisonburg

SHENANDOAH R.

Staunton

Fredericksburg

POTOMAC R.

Charlottesville

95

RAPPAHANNOCK R.

Chesapeake Bay

64

Lexington

JAMES RIVER

Richmond

64

ALLEGHENY MOUNTAINS

KY.

77

Roanoke

Lynchburg

Appomattox

Petersburg

York R.

64

Williamsburg

Pulaski

81

BLUE RIDGE MOUNTAINS

ROANOKE RIVER

85

Hampton

Newport News

ATLANTIC OCEAN

Wytheville

NEW RIVER

77

Buggs Island Lake

Lake Gaston

95

Norfolk

Virginia Beach

Bristol

Danville

Chesapeake

...VER

Great Dismal Swamp National Wildlife Refuge

TN.

Johnson City

NORTH CAROLINA

Raleigh

DID YOU KNOW?

that the Pentagon in Arlington, with 23,000 workers and 284 rest rooms, is one of the world's largest office buildings?

◄----- 440 miles (708 km) -----►

ABOUT VIRGINIA

NICKNAME: Old Dominion

CAPITAL: Richmond

STATEHOOD: June 25, 1788 (10th)

MOTTO: Thus always to tyrants.

POPULATION: 7,187,734 (12th)

AREA: 42,777 sq. mi. (35th)

(110,745 sq km)

HIGHEST POINT: 5,729 ft. (Mount Rogers)

LOWEST POINT: Sea level (Atlantic Ocean)

FLOWER: Flowering dogwood

TREE: Flowering dogwood

BIRD: Cardinal

Virginia

In George Washington's time, Virginia was a rich agricultural state. Today, however, farming is primarily confined to small family operations. The biggest employer now is the federal government, which accounts for nearly one fourth of the state's total income. The Hampton Roads naval base alone generates some seven billion dollars a year.

The people who live in Virginia's northern counties, many of whom commute to jobs in Washington, D.C., reflect the multicultural makeup of the nation's capital. On the other hand, Richmond still adheres to a recognizably southern way of life. In this regard, the former Confederate stronghold now forms a convenient bridge between North and South.

Like other southern seaboard states, Virginia slopes down from mountains in the west to marshland in the east. The most important ranges in Virginia, the Blue Ridge and Allegheny mountains, belong to the Appalachian chain. Below them lie the rolling hills of the Piedmont, which gradually descend to the fall line. Here the land "falls" abruptly to the Atlantic Coastal Plain, creating river rapids and waterfalls. (Many Virginia cities—including Alexandria, Fredericksburg, Richmond, and Petersburg—grew up along the fall line to take advantage of its cheap waterpower.) Finally, the low sandy plain surrounding Chesapeake Bay is called the Tidewater because of the effect that the ocean tides have on its inlets and waterways.

Virginia boasts an unusually large number of historic sites, from the homes of George Washington and Thomas Jefferson to important Revolutionary and Civil War battlefields. Among the most popular sites is Colonial Williamsburg, a restoration designed to show visitors the colonial capital as Washington and Jefferson knew it.

The twenty-three-mile-long (thirty-seven-kilometer-long) Chesapeake Bay Bridge-Tunnel connects the southern side of Hampton Roads with Virginia's Eastern Shore. The structure, the longest of its kind in the world, includes two bridges, four artificial islands, and a pair of tunnels that pass under the bay's two main shipping channels.

The scenic, fertile Shenandoah Valley lies between the Blue Ridge and Allegheny mountains. Its name, of Native American origin, means "daughter of the stars."

LEGEND

🛡20 Interstate Highways	⭐ State Capital	⬛ National Parks and Refuges	🌲 National Forests	▲ Highest Point	0 miles 50 / 0 kilometers 80

DID YOU KNOW?

that in West Virginia's thin northern panhandle the city of Weirton stretches across the entire state?

Pittsburgh

PENNSYLVANIA

Weirton

Wheeling

🛡70

OHIO

OHIO RIVER

Morgantown 🛡68

Fairmont

Clarksburg

Parkersburg

🛡79

MD.

Cumberland

NORTH BRANCH POTOMAC R.

Keyser

SOUTH BRANCH POTOMAC R.

POTOMAC R.

Hagerstown

Harpers Ferry National Historical Park

Martinsburg

🛡81

SHENANDOAH R.

Buckhannon

🛡79

Elkins

🛡77

KANAWHA R.

Sutton Lake

ELK RIVER

ALLEGHENY MOUNTAINS

Spruce Knob Seneca Rocks National Reservation Area

VIRGINIA

Charlottesville

OHIO RIVER

🛡64

Charleston

Huntington

BIG SANDY RIVER →

South Charleston

GAULEY RIVER

GUYANDOTTE RIVER

TUG FORK RIVER

🛡77 🛡64 • Oak Hill

Beckley

NEW RIVER

🛡64

KENTUCKY

🛡77

Bluefield

Roanoke

Since the nineteenth century, the health of West Virginia's economy has depended on coal mining. The huge seams of soft bituminous coal that underlie the state have made it the nation's second largest coal producer (behind Wyoming). Yet this dependence has also bound generations of West Virginians to hard, dangerous work in the mines.

◄———— **265 miles (426 km)** ————►

ABOUT WEST VIRGINIA

NICKNAME: Mountain State	**POPULATION:** 1,801,916 (37th)	**FLOWER:** Rhododendron
CAPITAL: Charleston	**AREA:** 24,231 sq. mi. (41st)	**TREE:** Sugar maple
STATEHOOD: June 20, 1863 (35th)	(62,731 sq km)	**BIRD:** Cardinal
MOTTO: Mountaineers are always free.	**HIGHEST POINT:** 4,861 ft. (Spruce Knob)	**FISH:** Brook trout
	LOWEST POINT: 240 ft. (Potomac River)	

West Virginia

Few states are as rugged as West Virginia. Except for a handful of floodplains surrounding its major rivers, there's almost no level ground. This makes farming difficult and frustrates all sorts of economic development because moving things around is so hard. As a result, West Virginia has remained a state of small, isolated communities tucked away in steep, narrow hollows. Only one in every three West Virginians lives in a city.

On the other hand, the mountains do supply West Virginia with the mineral wealth that is its main source of income. In addition to coal, West Virginians mine silica-rich sandstone for glassware (and most U.S. marbles), clay for pottery, and salt for dyes, paints, and plastics. The Native American word *kanawha*, meaning "place of the white stone," refers to the large deposits of salt in the Kanawha and Ohio river valleys.

Passing approximately through Elkins, the Allegheny Front separates the Allegheny Plateau, which covers the western two thirds of the state, from the Appalachian Ridge and Valley system in the east. Millions of years ago, the Allegheny Plateau was a high flatland, but over time rivers have eroded the softer rock, creating the present maze of hills and valleys.

Like most natives of Appalachia, West Virginians take great pride in their folk culture, especially the "mountain music" they play on fiddles, dulcimers, mandolins, and other homemade string instruments. Nationally syndicated *Mountain Stage,* produced by West Virginia Public Radio, features this music along with contemporary folk, blues, and even rock 'n' roll.

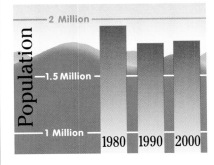

During the 1980s, West Virginia lost more population than any other state, falling from 1,950,186 residents in 1980 to 1,793,477 in 1990. Most of those who left were young people from rural areas who were having trouble finding jobs. Since 1992, the population has stabilized at about 1,800,000.

All of West Virginia lies within the Appalachian Mountains. The state's highest point is Spruce Knob, from whose summit this view was taken.

CANADA

LAKE SUPERIOR

Minnesota
page 72

Wisconsin
page 78

LAKE HURON

LAKE MICHIGAN

Michigan
page 70

LAKE ERIE

Iowa
page 68

MISSOURI RIVER

Ohio
page 76

WABASH RIVER

ILLINOIS RIVER

Illinois
page 64

Indiana
page 66

Missouri
page 74

MISSISSIPPI RIVER

OHIO RIVER

During the last Ice Age, huge glaciers covered nearly all the Midwest. Like unfrozen water, these glaciers also flowed, if very slowly. Their movement had the same effect as a giant bulldozer, flattening the land and leaving behind a thick layer of mixed clay and stone, called till. Most of this region now belongs to what geographers call the Dissected Till Plains. (*Dissected* means "cut up," referring in this case to the way that rivers and streams have cut up the tableland.)

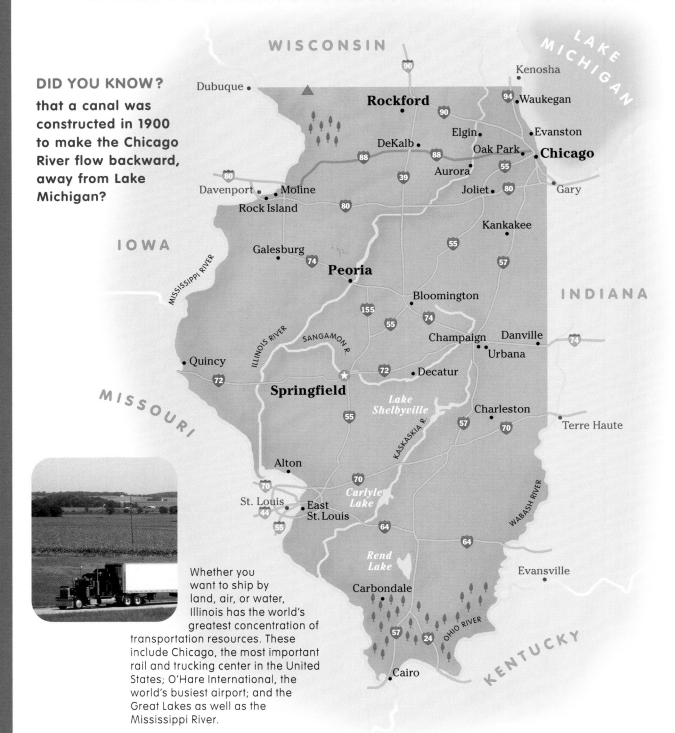

Interstate Highways

State Capital

National Forests

Highest Point

0	miles	50
0	kilometers	80

WISCONSIN

LAKE MICHIGAN

Dubuque

Kenosha

Rockford

Waukegan

DID YOU KNOW?

that a canal was constructed in 1900 to make the Chicago River flow backward, away from Lake Michigan?

Elgin

Evanston

DeKalb

Oak Park

Chicago

Aurora

Davenport

Moline

Joliet

Gary

Rock Island

IOWA

Kankakee

Galesburg

Peoria

Bloomington

INDIANA

MISSISSIPPI RIVER

ILLINOIS RIVER

SANGAMON R.

Champaign

Danville

Urbana

Quincy

Decatur

Springfield

Lake Shelbyville

Charleston

MISSOURI

Terre Haute

KASKASKIA R.

Alton

Carlyle Lake

WABASH RIVER

St. Louis

East St. Louis

Rend Lake

Evansville

Carbondale

KENTUCKY

OHIO RIVER

Cairo

Whether you want to ship by land, air, or water, Illinois has the world's greatest concentration of transportation resources. These include Chicago, the most important rail and trucking center in the United States; O'Hare International, the world's busiest airport; and the Great Lakes as well as the Mississippi River.

◄—————— 211 miles (339 km) ——————►

ABOUT ILLINOIS

NICKNAME: Prairie State

CAPITAL: Springfield

STATEHOOD: December 3, 1818 (21st)

MOTTO: State sovereignty—national union.

POPULATION: 12,482,301 (5th)

AREA: 57,918 sq. mi. (25th) (149,943 sq km)

HIGHEST POINT: 1,235 ft. (Charles Mound)

LOWEST POINT: 279 ft. (Mississippi River)

FLOWER: Native violet

TREE: White oak

BIRD: Cardinal

FISH: Bluegill

Illinois

ILLINOIS

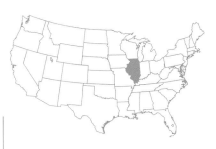

If you live in Illinois, you're either a Chicagoan or a downstater. Being a Chicagoan means that you live in the nation's third largest city or one of its many suburbs. Everyone else is a downstater. Because Chicagoans significantly outnumber downstaters in Illinois, they tend to monopolize state politics. Downstaters sometimes joke that Chicagoans believe their immediate neighbors are New York City and Los Angeles. Nevertheless, all Illinoisans take great pride in the fact that Abraham Lincoln spent his entire adult life in the state. (Interestingly, Lincoln lived in New Salem and later in Springfield, but never in Chicago.)

Overall, Chicago has benefited greatly from its central location and easy access to both the Great Lakes and the Mississippi River. Because the city is a major transportation hub, it can easily import raw materials and then ship out finished goods. This has helped it become a major U.S. manufacturing center, second only to the Los Angeles area in the number of manufacturing jobs it offers.

Unlike industrial Chicago, downstate Illinois is rural and agricultural. Primarily flat, with hilly areas only in the northwest and south, it lies almost entirely within the Dissected Till Plains, whose flat topography and rich glacial soil present ideal conditions for farming. As elsewhere in the midwestern farm belt, the major crops in Illinois are corn and soybeans.

Although blues originated among African Americans in the rural South about 1900, the music quickly migrated north along with southern blacks seeking industrial jobs. During the Great Depression, Big Bill Broonzy and Sonny Boy Williamson became popular performers in Chicago. After World War II, Muddy Waters, Elmore James, and Howlin' Wolf (pictured here) made Chicago-style urban blues world famous.

GLACIER

During the last Ice Age, glaciers covered nearly all of Illinois. These huge masses of ice flattened the state, grinding down hills and leaving behind a layer of mineral-rich soil. In other words, they turned Illinois into excellent farmland.

The skyscraper, first developed in Chicago, continues to dominate that city's skyline. Until the 1997 completion of the 1,483-foot (452-meter) Petronas Towers in Malaysia, the 1,450-foot (442-meter) Sears Tower was the world's tallest building.

Interstate Highways

State Capital

National Parks and Refuges

National Forests

Highest Point

0   miles   50
0   kilometers   80

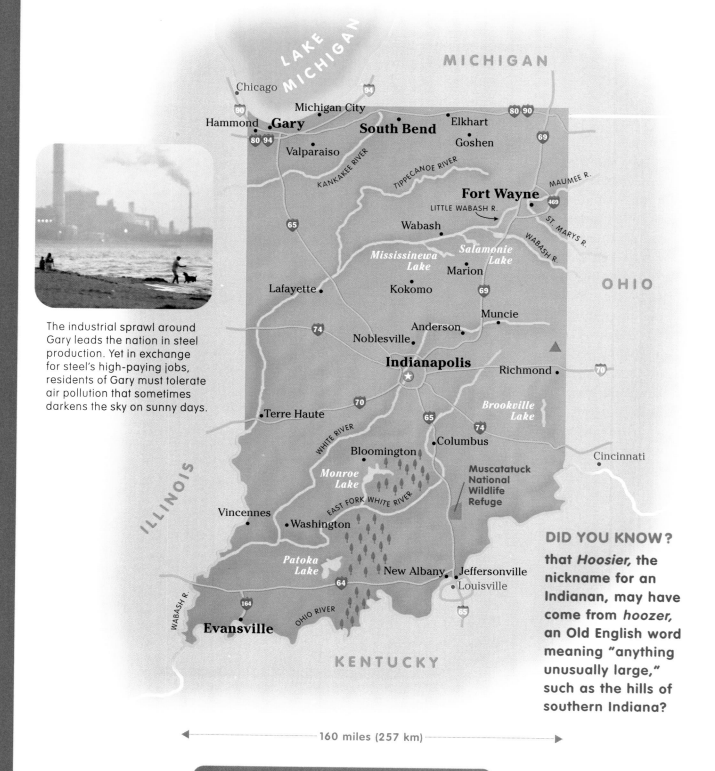

LAKE MICHIGAN

MICHIGAN

Chicago

Michigan City

Hammond   **Gary**

South Bend

Elkhart

Goshen

Valparaiso

KANKAKEE RIVER

TIPPECANOE RIVER

MAUMEE R.

Fort Wayne

LITTLE WABASH R.

ST. MARYS R.

WABASH R.

Wabash

Mississinewa Lake

Salamonie Lake

Marion

OHIO

Lafayette

Kokomo

Muncie

Anderson

Noblesville

Indianapolis

Richmond

Brookville Lake

Terre Haute

Columbus

Cincinnati

WHITE RIVER

Bloomington

Monroe Lake

Muscatatuck National Wildlife Refuge

ILLINOIS

EAST FORK WHITE RIVER

Vincennes

Washington

Patoka Lake

New Albany

Jeffersonville

Louisville

WABASH R.

Evansville

OHIO RIVER

KENTUCKY

The industrial sprawl around Gary leads the nation in steel production. Yet in exchange for steel's high-paying jobs, residents of Gary must tolerate air pollution that sometimes darkens the sky on sunny days.

DID YOU KNOW?
that *Hoosier,* the nickname for an Indianan, may have come from *hoozer,* an Old English word meaning "anything unusually large," such as the hills of southern Indiana?

← 160 miles (257 km) →

ABOUT INDIANA

NICKNAME: Hoosier State
CAPITAL: Indianapolis
STATEHOOD: December 11, 1816 (19th)
MOTTO: The crossroads of America.

POPULATION: 6,114,745 (14th)
AREA: 36,420 sq. mi. (38th)
(94,287 sq km)
HIGHEST POINT: 1,257 ft. (Franklin Township)
LOWEST POINT: 320 ft. (Ohio River)

FLOWER: Peony
TREE: Tulip tree
BIRD: Cardinal

Indiana

The landscape of Indiana, like that of Illinois and Iowa, was shaped by the glaciers that covered the Midwest during the last Ice Age. In the northern third of the state, these glaciers left behind many hollows that became kettle lakes. In central Indiana, they flattened the land and deposited a rocky debris called till. Over time, the sand, clay, and minerals that made up the till eroded into a thick layer of highly fertile soil. Only the southern sixth of Indiana, a region rich in coal and limestone, escaped the glaciers, and so only its hills were preserved.

Farms established on Indiana's central flatlands flourished during the nineteenth century. Since 1900, however, manufacturing has become increasingly important to the state, particularly in its northwestern corner, which abuts Lake Michigan. Gary, for example, became a popular location for steel plants because it lay halfway between the iron ranges of Minnesota and the coalfields of southern Indiana.

The population of Indiana is only 8 percent black. Yet the city of Gary is 84 percent black because nearly all the blacks in Indiana live there—or in Fort Wayne or Indianapolis. The rest of the state, except for a large Polish community in South Bend, is typically white, Protestant, and English, Irish, or German in descent.

No sport arouses the passion of Hoosiers the way that basketball does. That's why the state's annual high school basketball tournament is called Hoosier Hysteria. Perhaps basketball, a winter sport, is especially popular in Indiana, a farming state, because it doesn't have to compete with spring planting or the fall harvest season.

Where Have All the Forests Gone?

When white settlers first came to Indiana during the early nineteenth century, about 80 percent of the state was covered with trees, especially beeches, sycamores, oaks, and maples. Then these pioneers began clearing the land for farms. Today, only 16 percent of Indiana remains forested.

Indiana limestone has been used to face the Empire State Building, the Pentagon, and many other celebrated structures. Workers in the quarries around Bloomington, which produce the finest limestone, are called cutters.

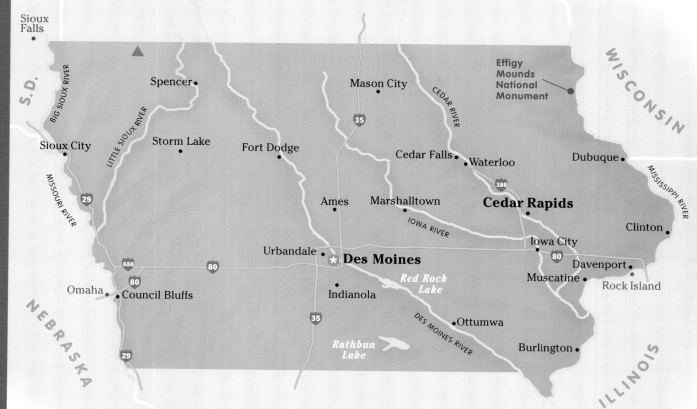

Interstate Highways
State Capital
National Parks and Refuges
Highest Point

| 0 | miles | 50 |
| 0 | kilometers | 80 |

DID YOU KNOW?

that nearly nine out of ten Iowans graduate from high school (compared to seven out of ten nationwide)?

MINNESOTA

Sioux Falls

S.D.

BIG SIOUX RIVER

Spencer

Mason City

Effigy Mounds National Monument

WISCONSIN

35

Sioux City

LITTLE SIOUX RIVER

Storm Lake

Fort Dodge

Cedar Falls
Waterloo

CEDAR RIVER

Dubuque

MISSISSIPPI RIVER

MISSOURI RIVER

29

Ames
Marshalltown

Cedar Rapids

380

Clinton

IOWA RIVER

680

Urbandale

80

Des Moines

Iowa City

80

Davenport

Muscatine

Rock Island

Omaha
Council Bluffs

80

29

Indianola

Red Rock Lake

35

Rathbun Lake

DES MOINES RIVER

Ottumwa

Burlington

ILLINOIS

NEBRASKA

MISSOURI

Most Iowans work in jobs related to farming. Although just 4 percent actually farm the land, many more have jobs in food-processing plants or factories making farm equipment. Waterloo has meat-packing and tractor plants, Cedar Rapids and Keokuk have large cereal mills, and Sioux City has the world's largest popcorn factory (pictured here).

324 miles (521 km)

ABOUT IOWA

NICKNAME: Hawkeye State
CAPITAL: Des Moines
STATEHOOD: December 28, 1846 (29th)
MOTTO: Our liberties we prize and our rights we will maintain.

POPULATION: 2,923,179 (30th)
AREA: 56,276 sq. mi. (26th)
(145,692 sq km)
HIGHEST POINT: 1,670 ft. (Ocheyedan Mound)
LOWEST POINT: 480 ft. (Mississippi River)

FLOWER: Wild rose
TREE: Oak
BIRD: Eastern goldfinch

Iowa

Iowa's greatest resource is its fertile soil. Like that in the rest of the midwestern farm belt, Iowa's soil was deposited by glaciers that once covered the entire state. Now farms cover 92 percent of the land, producing one fifth of the nation's corn and also a fifth of its hogs.

Following a national trend, farms in Iowa have been increasing in size while decreasing in number. The cause of this has been large agricultural corporations buying up and merging small family spreads. In 1955, there were 193,000 farms in Iowa; today, there are merely half that number. Many small farmers, unable to compete, have gone bankrupt, threatening Iowa's small-town way of life. One way that the state has sought to stabilize its economy during bad farm cycles has been to encourage nonfarm industries, such as computer manufacturing in Cedar Rapids and insurance in Des Moines.

Most people think of Iowa as pancake flat, and central Iowa certainly is, but other parts of the state are hilly. In the northeastern corner, for instance, streams have eroded the bedrock to form rugged valleys. In fact, some of the bluffs lining the Mississippi River are four hundred feet (120 m) high. In the west, however, the hills bordering the Missouri River Valley are not uneroded bedrock but accumulations of windblown silt called loess.

Because Iowa is a state of small towns, it can't support the same cultural institutions, such as symphonies and museums, that states with large cities can. Instead, cultural life in Iowa is often centered on colleges and universities, such as the University of Iowa, which runs the prestigious Iowa Writers' Workshop.

The Uniform State

Because Iowa has an evenly distributed population and very few minorities (only 6 percent of the population), social scientists often use it as an example of "large-scale uniformity." This means that, compared to other states, Iowans are very much alike.

Each of Iowa's small towns is often little more than a few houses, some grain elevators, and a church. Most Iowans say they prefer life on that scale. Yet more and more have been forced by farm failures to take jobs in the cities.

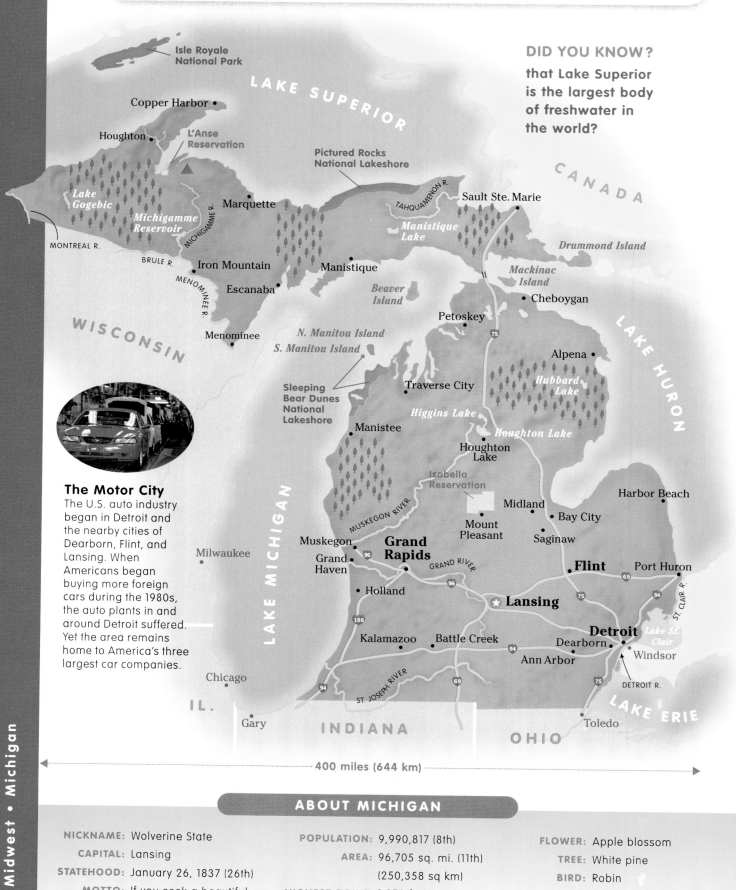

LEGEND

Interstate Highways	
State Capital	
Native American Reservations	
National Forests	
National Parks and Refuges	
Highest Point	

0 miles 50
0 kilometers 80

Isle Royale National Park

LAKE SUPERIOR

Copper Harbor •

Houghton •

L'Anse Reservation

Lake Gogebic

Michigamme Reservoir

MONTREAL R.

BRULE R.

MICHIGAMME R.

Marquette •

Pictured Rocks National Lakeshore

TAHQUAMENON R.

Sault Ste. Marie

CANADA

Manistique Lake

Drummond Island

DID YOU KNOW?
that Lake Superior is the largest body of freshwater in the world?

Iron Mountain •

MENOMINEE R.

Escanaba •

Menominee •

WISCONSIN

Manistique •

Beaver Island

N. Manitou Island
S. Manitou Island

Sleeping Bear Dunes National Lakeshore

Mackinac Island

Cheboygan •

Petoskey •

Alpena •

Hubbard Lake

75

Traverse City •

Higgins Lake

Houghton Lake

LAKE HURON

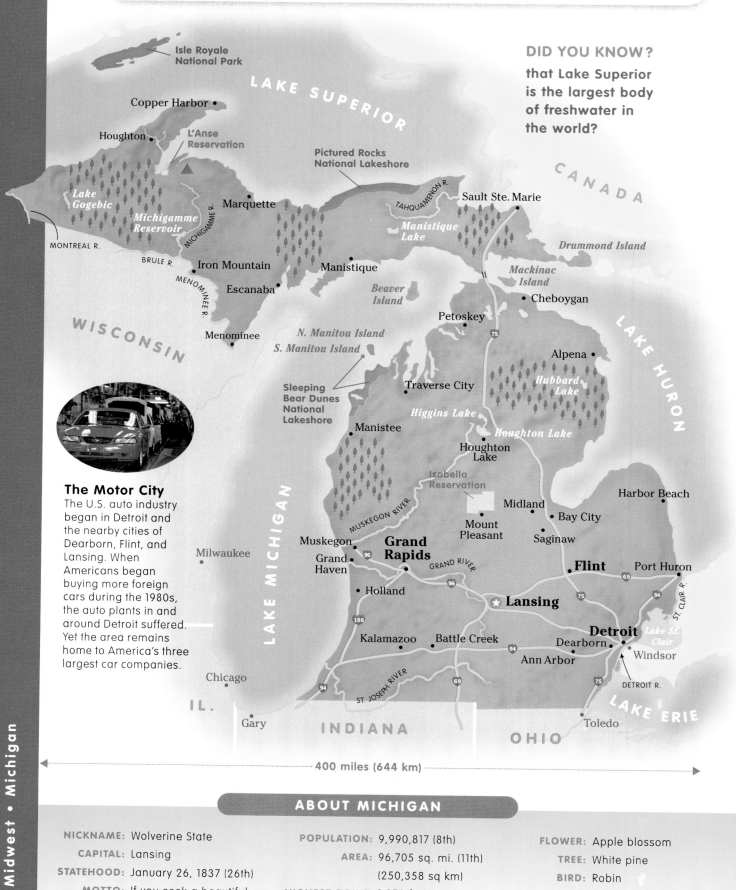

The Motor City
The U.S. auto industry began in Detroit and the nearby cities of Dearborn, Flint, and Lansing. When Americans began buying more foreign cars during the 1980s, the auto plants in and around Detroit suffered. Yet the area remains home to America's three largest car companies.

Manistee •

MUSKEGON RIVER

Isabella Reservation

Houghton Lake •

Mount Pleasant •

Midland •

Bay City •

Saginaw •

Harbor Beach

Muskegon •

Grand Haven •

Grand Rapids

95

GRAND RIVER

Flint

Port Huron

69

ST. CLAIR R.

Milwaukee •

LAKE MICHIGAN

Holland •

96

★ **Lansing**

75

94

Detroit

Lake St. Clair

Windsor

196

Kalamazoo •

Battle Creek •

Dearborn •

Ann Arbor •

Chicago •

94

69

94

St. JOSEPH RIVER

75

DETROIT R.

LAKE ERIE

Gary •

IL.

INDIANA

OHIO

Toledo •

← 400 miles (644 km) →

ABOUT MICHIGAN

NICKNAME: Wolverine State
CAPITAL: Lansing
STATEHOOD: January 26, 1837 (26th)
MOTTO: If you seek a beautiful peninsula, look around you.

POPULATION: 9,990,817 (8th)
AREA: 96,705 sq. mi. (11th)
(250,358 sq km)
HIGHEST POINT: 1,979 ft. (Mount Arvon)
LOWEST POINT: 571 ft. (Lake Erie)

FLOWER: Apple blossom
TREE: White pine
BIRD: Robin
FISH: Brook trout

Michigan

A peninsula is a spit of land, shaped like a tongue, bounded on three sides by water. The state of Michigan is actually a pair of peninsulas, one divided from the other by the Straits of Mackinac (pronounced MACK-i-naw). Michigan's sometimes hilly, sometimes swampy Upper Peninsula is connected to the flatter, mitten-shaped Lower Peninsula by the Mackinac Bridge.

Michigan is called the Great Lakes State because it borders four of the five Great Lakes. As a result, shipping has always been an important business there. The locks at Sault Ste. Marie (nicknamed "the Soo") were opened in 1855 to service ships carrying timber and iron ore from Minnesota and the Upper Peninsula. These locks, which equalize the water level between Lake Superior and Lake Huron, are still among the world's busiest.

Michiganders in great numbers also use the Great Lakes for recreation. The rural Upper Peninsula doesn't have many people, but most of them fish. So do the carloads of Detroiters and Chicagoans who visit the Upper Peninsula each summer for a vacation out-of-doors. Despite the fact that it contains every one of Michigan's major cities and important industrial centers, the Lower Peninsula is no less outdoorsy. In fact, Michiganders of both peninsulas own more boats than residents of any other state.

The fish boil has been a Great Lakes tradition since the nineteenth century. It was devised by Scandinavian immigrants who wanted an easy way to cook whitefish and lake trout. For a traditional outdoor fish boil, Michiganders cook chunks of fish, potatoes, and onions in seasoned water over large wood fires.

75%

Michigan's Slice of the Pie
Michigan produces about 75 percent of the sour pie cherries grown in the United States. The area around Traverse City is particularly good for growing cherries because Lake Michigan moderates the weather there, tempering the frosts and cooling the orchards during summer.

Large ships haul cargo from the Midwest to the East (and beyond) using the St. Lawrence Seaway. This system of canals, locks, and dams joins the Great Lakes to the Atlantic Ocean.

LEGEND

Interstate Highways | State Capital | Native American Reservations | National Forests | National Parks and Refuges | Marshlands | Highest Point

0 — miles — 50
0 — kilometers — 80

The Mesabi Range once produced more than half the world's iron ore. The richest deposits have long been depleted, but the area around Hibbing still fills about two thirds of the U.S. need with a plentiful low-grade ore called taconite. Mining companies get at the taconite by stripping away the thin soil and digging large open pits.

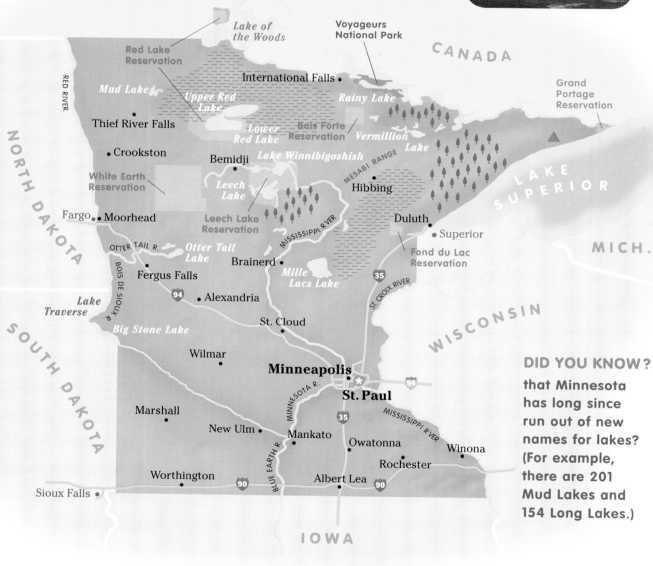

CANADA

Lake of the Woods

Voyageurs National Park

Red Lake Reservation

International Falls

Grand Portage Reservation

RED RIVER

Mud Lake

Upper Red Lake

Rainy Lake

Thief River Falls

Bois Forte Reservation

Vermillion Lake

Lower Red Lake

Crookston

Bemidji

Lake Winnibigoshish

MESABI RANGE

LAKE SUPERIOR

White Earth Reservation

Leech Lake

Hibbing

Fargo • Moorhead

Leech Lake Reservation

Duluth

MISSISSIPPI RIVER

Superior

MICH.

OTTER TAIL R.

Otter Tail Lake

Fond du Lac Reservation

BOIS DE SIOUX R.

Brainerd

Fergus Falls

Mille Lacs Lake

35

ST. CROIX RIVER

Lake Traverse

94

Alexandria

St. Cloud

WISCONSIN

Big Stone Lake

Wilmar

Minneapolis

St. Paul

94

Marshall

MINNESOTA R.

New Ulm

Mankato

35

MISSISSIPPI RIVER

Owatonna

Winona

BLUE EARTH R.

Worthington

Rochester

Albert Lea

90

90

Sioux Falls

NORTH DAKOTA

SOUTH DAKOTA

IOWA

DID YOU KNOW?
that Minnesota has long since run out of new names for lakes? (For example, there are 201 Mud Lakes and 154 Long Lakes.)

← 358 miles (576 km) →

ABOUT MINNESOTA

NICKNAME: Gopher State
CAPITAL: St. Paul
STATEHOOD: May 11, 1858 (32nd)
MOTTO: Star of the North.

POPULATION: 4,972,294 (21st)
AREA: 86,943 sq. mi. (12th)
(225,085 sq km)
HIGHEST POINT: 2,301 ft. (Eagle Mountain)
LOWEST POINT: 600 ft. (Lake Superior)

FLOWER: Pink and white lady's slipper
TREE: Norway pine
BIRD: Common loon
FISH: Walleye

Minnesota

More than half of Minnesota's population lives in or near the Twin Cities of Minneapolis and St. Paul, built along the Mississippi River at the head of its navigable waters. Indeed, the Twin Cities are the largest metropolitan area for hundreds of miles around. As a result, they've become an important transportation, business, and cultural center for the entire upper Midwest.

Minneapolis and St. Paul are such cosmopolitan cities that a minority presence there doesn't seem unusual, yet that isn't the case elsewhere in Minnesota. Overwhelmingly, Minnesota's residents are white, mostly of German and Scandinavian descent, accounting for 93 percent of the population statewide. Even in a city such as Duluth, all the minorities taken together account for just 4 percent of the population.

Minnesota calls itself the Land of Ten Thousand Lakes, even though there are more than fifteen thousand of them. Most were left behind when the midwestern glaciers receded after the last Ice Age. In the Mesabi Range, those glaciers bulldozed away rock covering large iron ore deposits. Elsewhere, they dumped the same rich soil that makes Iowa farmland so fertile. Not surprisingly, mining and dairying have both become important industries in the state. Minnesota's dairy cows rank among the national leaders in butter production, while Duluth remains one of the world's busiest freshwater ports, largely because of iron ore and grain shipments.

What most Americans know about Minnesota, true or not, they probably learned from Garrison Keillor, host of *A Prairie Home Companion.* Keillor's weekly radio variety show, broadcast live from St. Paul, features "The News from Lake Wobegon," an account of recent events in Keillor's imaginary hometown "where all the children are above average."

to Hudson Bay

to Atlantic Ocean

to Gulf of Mexico

Minnesota straddles three continental watersheds. Southern Minnesota drains into the Mississippi River (and thereby the Gulf of Mexico). In the west, the Red River flows north toward Canada's Hudson Bay. In the northeast, the region around Duluth drains into the Atlantic Ocean via Lake Superior.

Canoeing is particularly popular in Minnesota, especially along the upper Mississippi River. The source of the Mississippi can be found at Lake Itasca, near Bemidji.

Interstate Highways · State Capital · National Parks and Refuges · National Forests · Highest Point

| 0 | miles | 50 |
| 0 | kilometers | 80 |

Among the most important of Missouri's diverse industries is the manufacture of transportation equipment. Missourians make automobiles, limousines, railroad cars, aircraft, and even spacecraft. Workers at the factory pictured here assemble fire engines.

IOWA

Squaw Creek National Wildlife Refuge

NEB.

• Maryville

29   35

• St. Joseph

DES MOINES R.

• Kirksville

CHARITON RIVER

GRAND RIVER

Hannibal •

Mark Twain Lake

ILLINOIS

Springfield

MISSOURI RIVER

Topeka
•

70

Independence

Kansas City

Sedalia
•

Columbia
•

70

St. Charles
•

55

70

Jefferson City ☆

MISSOURI RIVER

St. Louis

35

Washington
•

64

KANSAS

Harry S. Truman Reservoir

Lake of the Ozarks

OSAGE RIVER

MISSISSIPPI RIVER

Nevada
•

Stockton Lake

44

Rolla
•

Farmington
•

55

Cape Girardeau
•

Cairo
•

Springfield

CURRENT RIVER

Big Spring
•

ST. FRANCIS RIVER

Joplin
•

OZARK MTS.

• West Plains

57

KY.

Table Rock Lake

Branson
•

Bull Shoals Lake

Poplar Bluff
•

WHITE RIVER

OKLAHOMA

ARKANSAS

TENN.

DID YOU KNOW?

that the town of Washington is the world's leading manufacturer of corncob pipes?

← 284 miles (457 km) →

ABOUT MISSOURI

NICKNAME: Show Me State

CAPITAL: Jefferson City

STATEHOOD: August 10, 1821 (24th)

MOTTO: Let the welfare of the people be the supreme law.

POPULATION: 5,629,707 (17th)

AREA: 69,709 sq. mi. (21st) (180,468 sq km)

HIGHEST POINT: 1,772 ft. (Taum Sauk Mt.)

LOWEST POINT: 230 ft. (St. Francis River)

FLOWER: Hawthorn

TREE: Flowering dogwood

BIRD: Bluebird

Missouri

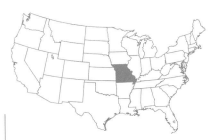

From any map it's easy to tell that the path of the Missouri River determined settlement patterns in the state: St. Louis, for example, was founded near the point at which the Missouri flows into the Mississippi, while Kansas City was built at the junction of the Missouri and Kansas rivers.

River transportation, once the state's most important business, has declined since the end of the nineteenth century, yet St. Louis has remained a national crossroads and midwestern cultural center, home to academically superior Washington University as well as a nationally respected symphony orchestra and art museum. Although the Catholic church in St. Louis isn't as vital as it once was, the city remains important enough to American Catholicism that it received a rare papal visit in 1999.

Topographically, Missouri is the most diverse state in the Midwest. The Missouri River marks the southernmost reach of the glaciers that once covered the region. (In fact, the Missouri's channel was carved by glacial meltwater running southeast into the Mississippi.) The land north of the Missouri, with its flattened contours and fertile glacial soil, belongs to the Corn Belt. South of the Missouri rise the forested hills and low mountains of the Ozark Plateau. In western Missouri, the prairies of the Great Plains begin, while in the southeastern corner of the state, in an area called the Bootheel, farmers till the rich bottomlands of the Mississippi floodplain.

Show Me
In 1899, Missouri congressman Willard D. Vandiver told an audience in Philadelphia, "I'm from Missouri. You've got to show me." That attitude of intelligent skepticism was later raised to a mythic level by Independence native Harry Truman, who as president kept on his White House desk a famous sign that read, I'M FROM MISSOURI.

27 ft (8 m)

Quite a Big Spring
Underground rivers in the Ozarks have, over time, eaten away large sections of the limestone bedrock, creating some of the biggest springs in the world. Big Spring, the nation's largest, pumps about 11.5 million gallons (43.5 million l) of water into the Current River each hour. That's enough flow to cover a football field with a column of water twenty-seven feet deep.

The 630-foot-tall (192-meter-tall) Gateway Arch celebrates St. Louis's role as the primary nineteenth-century transportation link between the East and the West. Today, St. Louis remains a key trucking and shipping center.

75

Interstate
Highways

State
Capital

National
Parks and Refuges

National
Forests

Highest Point

0   miles   50
0   kilometers   80

Every summer, Akron hosts the All-American Soap Box Derby. For more than a century, Akron led the world in tire research and production. Then foreign competitors caught up, and people began buying tires made elsewhere. Akron's city leaders are now searching for another industry to take rubber's place.

Detroit

CANADA

LAKE ERIE

Erie

MICHIGAN

Ashtabula

Pymatuning Reservoir

Kelleys Island

Euclid

Cleveland

Toledo

90

Sandusky   Lorain

MAUMEE RIVER

Bowling Green

80 90

CUYAHOGA R.

Mosquito Creek Lake

Defiance

80 90

77

271

80

Warren

Fort Wayne

Findlay

Tiffin

71

Kent

Youngstown

ST. MARYS R.

75

SANDUSKY R.

76

Akron

Lima

Ashland

Massillon   Canton

Indian Lake

Mansfield

INDIANA

Lake St. Marys

Marion

Millersburg

GREAT MIAMI RIVER

71

77

Steubenville

PENN.

Columbus

Newark

70

70

Zanesville

Springfield

MUSKINGUM RIVER

70

Dayton

71

Lancaster

77

Middletown

75

Mound City Group National Monument

Hamilton

OHIO RIVER

Chillicothe

Athens

SCIOTO RIVER

Cincinnati

WEST VIRGINIA

71

75

OHIO RIVER

Portsmouth

DID YOU KNOW?

that the McDonald's in heavily Amish Millersburg has a drive-through window at buggy height?

KENTUCKY

←—————— 210 miles (338 km) ——————→

ABOUT OHIO

NICKNAME: Buckeye State
CAPITAL: Columbus
STATEHOOD: March 1, 1803 (17th)
MOTTO: With God, all things are possible.

POPULATION: 11,373,541 (7th)
AREA: 44,828 sq. mi. (34th)
(116,054 sq km)
HIGHEST POINT: 1,549 ft. (Campbell Hill)
LOWEST POINT: 455 ft. (Ohio River)

FLOWER: Scarlet carnation
TREE: Buckeye
BIRD: Cardinal

Ohio

Ohio is easy to cross, which is why most nineteenth-century pioneers passed through it on their journeys west. The state contains no natural barriers, such as deserts or mountain ranges, to make travel difficult. Of course, the Allegheny Plateau, covering eastern Ohio, has some rough hills and deep valleys, but beyond the Scioto River, the rest of the state is just gently rolling farmland. If you prefer water travel, Lake Erie and the Ohio River both provide excellent transportation routes. Every day, ships and barges make extensive use of these waterways, carrying raw materials to (and finished products from) Ohio's many factories. Because of these factories, Ohio ranks third in manufacturing jobs, trailing only California and Texas.

Between 1850 and 1950, Ohio's steel and machine-tool industries created good jobs that attracted immigrants from all over the world. Cleveland, for example, has had neighborhoods devoted to Germans, Irish, Poles, Italians, Czechs, Russians, Greeks, and also blacks who moved up from the South after the Civil War. However, as industry in Ohio grew unchecked, so did the presence of black smoke in the air and harmful chemicals in the water. Now that heavy industry in Ohio has declined, as it has elsewhere in the region, Ohioans must contend with the twin problems of pollution and unemployment.

One of the most unusual groups to have settled in Ohio are the Amish. A highly religious people, the Amish are known for their rejection of modern conveniences, such as cars and electricity, and for their excellent farming skills. Although many Amish live in Pennsylvania, the nation's largest Amish community is located in Holmes County near Millersburg.

Ohio lies at the eastern end of the agricultural Corn Belt that stretches all the way west to Nebraska. Known to geographers as the Dissected Till Plains, this region was created thousands of years ago by glaciers that flattened the land and left behind fertile soil when they melted.

During the 1960s, the pollution became so bad in Lake Erie that it was declared "dead." Since then, environmental laws have stopped the dumping of untreated chemicals. As a result, fish have returned, and beaches have been reopened.

LEGEND

Interstate Highways — 20
State Capital — ★
Native American Reservations — ▢
National Forests — ⬆⬆⬆
National Parks and Refuges — ▪
Highest Point — ▲

0 — miles — 50
0 — kilometers — 80

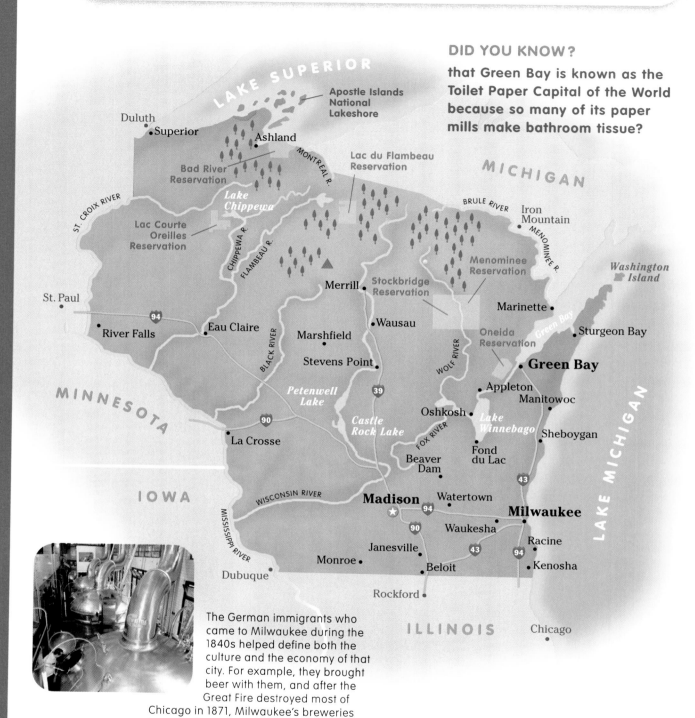

DID YOU KNOW?

that Green Bay is known as the Toilet Paper Capital of the World because so many of its paper mills make bathroom tissue?

LAKE SUPERIOR

Apostle Islands National Lakeshore

Duluth
• Superior
Ashland

Bad River Reservation
MONTREAL R.

Lac du Flambeau Reservation

MICHIGAN

BRULE RIVER
Iron Mountain

ST. CROIX RIVER
Lake Chippewa

MENOMINEE R.

Lac Courte Oreilles Reservation

CHIPPEWA R.
FLAMBEAU R.

Menominee Reservation

Washington Island

St. Paul

Merrill
Stockbridge Reservation

Marinette •

• River Falls
94
Eau Claire •
Marshfield •
• Wausau

Oneida Reservation

• Sturgeon Bay

MINNESOTA

WOLF RIVER

Green Bay

Green Bay

Stevens Point •

• Appleton

• Manitowoc

Petenwell Lake
39
Oshkosh •
Lake Winnebago

Castle Rock Lake
90
• La Crosse

FOX RIVER
Fond du Lac

Sheboygan

Beaver Dam

IOWA
WISCONSIN RIVER

MISSISSIPPI RIVER

Madison ★
94
Watertown •

Milwaukee
43

90
Waukesha •

Monroe •
Janesville •
43
Racine

LAKE MICHIGAN

Dubuque •
Beloit •
94
• Kenosha

Rockford •

ILLINOIS

Chicago

The German immigrants who came to Milwaukee during the 1840s helped define both the culture and the economy of that city. For example, they brought beer with them, and after the Great Fire destroyed most of Chicago in 1871, Milwaukee's breweries became the nation's most important.

◄———————— 295 miles (475 km) ————————►

ABOUT WISCONSIN

NICKNAME: Badger State
CAPITAL: Madison
STATEHOOD: May 29, 1848 (30th)
MOTTO: Forward.

POPULATION: 5,401,906 (18th)
AREA: 65,499 sq. mi. (23rd)
(169,569 sq km)
HIGHEST POINT: 1,951 ft. (Timms Hill)
LOWEST POINT: 579 ft. (Lake Michigan)

FLOWER: Wood violet
TREE: Sugar maple
BIRD: Robin
FISH: Muskellunge

Wisconsin

Wisconsin calls itself America's Dairyland with good reason: Its 1.3 million dairy cows are the most of any state. "Milking" this advantage, Wisconsin leads the nation in both butter and cheese making and places second (behind California) in overall milk production.

Most of Wisconsin's dairy farms are located in the southern two-thirds of the state. During the last Ice Age, glaciers flattened this area and enriched its soil. Curiously, though, the glaciers flowed around southwestern Wisconsin, creating a Driftless Area of steep valleys and narrow ridges that extends into Minnesota, Iowa, and Illinois. (Drift is glacial debris.) In the north, Wisconsin is mostly forested with second-growth trees that grew up naturally after older ones were cut down by settlers or harvested by paper companies.

Wisconsin's manufacturing industries and largest cities are concentrated in the southeast. The state's most successful paper mills, for example, are in the Fox and Wisconsin river valleys. Southeastern Wisconsin is also filled with many ethnic enclaves that reflect the state's history of heavy immigration from northern Europe. The Germans who arrived first were soon followed by Poles, Swedes, and Norwegians, among other groups. Today, Wisconsinites celebrate their cultural heritage with such annual events as the Wilhelm Tell Festival in New Glarus (Swiss), the Syttende Mai Festival in Stoughton (Norwegian), and the Fyr Bal Festival in Ephraim (Icelandic).

What the Kentucky Derby is to horse racing, the Oshkosh Fly-In is to aviation. Every summer, pilots from all over the world descend on Wittman Regional Airport in Oshkosh, flying more than ten thousand small aircraft. The occasion is the annual convention of the Experimental Aircraft Association.

Nearly 90 percent of the state's milk goes to cheese making, an industry promoted in Wisconsin by German, Swiss, and Norwegian immigrants more than a century ago.

The lakes and forests of Wisconsin's North Woods attract hunters and fishermen from all over the Midwest. Much of the land is protected by Wisconsin's environmental laws, among the most progressive in the nation.

North Dakota
page 86

YELLOWSTONE RIVER

South Dakota
page 88

Nebraska
page 84

SOUTH PLATTE RIVER

PLATTE RIVER

MISSOURI RIVER

Kansas
page 82

ARKANSAS RIVER

Great Plains

W ith no large body of water nearby to moderate the climate, the landlocked states of the Great Plains enjoy (or suffer from) some of the nation's most extreme weather. The summers are hot, the winters are cold and snowy, and the wind blows mightily year-round because there are few natural barriers (such as trees or hills) to block it. During spring and fall when air masses clash overhead, violent weather often results, and tornadoes are common.

LEGEND

🛣 20 Interstate Highways   ⭐ State Capital   ◻ Native American Reservations   ◼ National Parks and Refuges   🔺 Highest Point

| 0 | miles | 100 |
| 0 | kilometers | 161 |

DID YOU KNOW?

that the first newspaper in Kansas was published in the Shawnee language?

NEBRASKA

Lincoln

MISSOURI

REPUBLICAN RIVER

Lebanon

Waconda Lake

Kickapoo Reservation

MISSOURI R.

Potowatomi Reservation

Atchison

Goodland

SMOKY HILLS

SOLOMON RIVER

Tuttle Creek Lake

Leavenworth

29

35

Milford Lake

Manhattan

KANSAS R.

Kansas City

70

SALINE RIVER

Hays

Junction City

Topeka

70

Lawrence

Kansas City

SMOKY HILL RIVER

Salina

Abilene

335

Olathe

70

Cedar Bluff Reservoir

Cheyenne Bottoms

Emporia

35

John Redmond Reservoir

Great Bend

McPherson

135

Quivira National Wildlife Refuge

Newton

35

Fort Scott

Garden City

Hutchinson

Cheney Reservoir

Wichita

NEOSHOE RIVER

ARKANSAS RIVER

Dodge City

Pratt

FLINT HILLS

Ulysses

Wellington

Winfield

Coffeyville

CIMARRON RIVER

RED HILLS

Arkansas City

35

Liberal

COL.

OKLAHOMA

Tulsa

Wichita-area companies such as Raytheon and Learjet lead the world in the manufacture of light aircraft, making nearly two out of every three planes sold. Referring to his factory's midcountry location, aircraft executive Walter Beech once said, "No matter where you deliver an airplane from Wichita, you're already halfway there."

← 411 miles (661 km) →

ABOUT KANSAS

NICKNAME: Sunflower State

CAPITAL: Topeka

STATEHOOD: January 29, 1861 (34th)

MOTTO: To the stars through difficulties.

POPULATION: 2,694,641 (32nd)

AREA: 82,282 sq. mi. (15th) (213,018 sq km)

HIGHEST POINT: 4,039 ft. (Mount Sunflower)

LOWEST POINT: 679 ft. (Verdigris River)

FLOWER: Wild native sunflower

TREE: Cottonwood

BIRD: Western meadowlark

Kansas

Kansas seems to encourage misconceptions. For example, early pioneers believed that its dry, hard soil could never be farmed. Yet in 1874, a group of Russian Mennonite immigrants introduced a special strain of hardy winter wheat that required much less water than other wheats. This Turkey Red strain transformed Kansas into the nation's leading wheat producer.

Another misconception is that Kansas is primarily an agricultural state. That may once have been true, but modern methods of farming —especially the expensive new machinery that allows fewer and fewer people to farm more and more land—have undermined the state's small-town way of life. Looking elsewhere for work, many young families have left western and central Kansas for the industrialized eastern third of the state. This shift has left Kansas's small towns smaller and the average age of the people who live in them higher.

Some people even think that Kansas is flat! In fact, much of the state is covered with low hills. The Dissected Till Plains of northeastern Kansas and the Osage Plains in the extreme southeast are both areas of rolling hills and rich prairie soil. West of the Osage Plains are the Flint Hills, whose abundant bluestem grass provides some of the best grazing land in the country. Farther west are the gently rising Great Plains, which take up half of the state beginning near Tuttle Creek in the north and Hutchinson in the south.

During the early twentieth century, when William Allen White edited the *Emporia Gazette,* Kansas became internationally famous for its many excellent small-town newspapers. Even today, Kansas has more newspapers per capita than any other state.

Truly Middle America
A limestone monument in a pasture just northeast of Lebanon marks the geographic center of the continental United States.

Although the wheat fields of central Kansas produce 15-20 percent of the annual U.S. harvest, farmers in the state make about twice as much money raising beef cattle in the Flint Hills and elsewhere.

LEGEND

🛣️ 20	⭐	⬜	🌲	⬛	🌿	🔺	0	miles	100
Interstate Highways	State Capital	Native American Reservations	National Forests	National Parks and Refuges	Grasslands	Highest Point	0	kilometers	161

DID YOU KNOW?

that Interstate 80, which follows the same route taken by the Oregon Trail and the first transcontinental railroad, remains the nation's busiest east-west highway?

SOUTH DAKOTA

IOWA

Oglala National Grassland

• Chadron

Valentine

MISSOURI RIVER

NIOBRARA RIVER

Santee Sioux Reservation

Sioux City

WY.

SAND HILLS

Valentine National Wildlife Refuge

ELKHORN RIVER

South Sioux City

Omaha Reservation

Alliance

Scottsbluff

Crescent Lake National Wildlife Refuge

Norfolk

NORTH PLATTE RIVER

Lake McConaughy

Broken Bow

LOUP RIVER

Columbus

Fremont

Omaha

Sidney

North Platte

PLATTE RIVER

Council Bluffs

Bellevue

Grand Island

80

Lincoln

SOUTH PLATTE RIVER

PLATTE RIVER

Kearney

Nebraska City

MISSOURI RIVER

COLORADO

McCook

Hastings

REPUBLICAN RIVER

Fairbury

• Beatrice

MO.

KANSAS

Although agriculture remains important to Nebraskans, the state economy has diversified in recent years. For example, Omaha was once a national center for meatpacking. Now the most prosperous companies in town are insurance companies and telemarketers.

◄——————————— 415 miles (668 km) ———————————►

ABOUT NEBRASKA

NICKNAME: Cornhusker State	**POPULATION:** 1,713,235 (38th)	**FLOWER:** Goldenrod
CAPITAL: Lincoln	**AREA:** 77,358 sq. mi. (16th)	**TREE:** Cottonwood
STATEHOOD: March 1, 1867 (37th)	(200,271 sq km)	**BIRD:** Western meadowlark
MOTTO: Equality before the law.	**HIGHEST POINT:** 5,424 ft. (Johnson Township)	
	LOWEST POINT: 840 ft. (Missouri River)	

Nebraska

The nineteenth-century homesteaders who settled Nebraska came out west to farm. At first, they concentrated themselves in the Platte River Valley, along the route of the Oregon Trail, where water was readily available. Then, as the use of irrigation expanded, they settled other parts of the state, once considered a Great American Desert by early explorers.

Today, agriculture has become such a universal way of life in Nebraska that farms and ranches occupy 94 percent of the land, the highest percentage of any state. In western Nebraska, wheat fields flow uninterrupted to the horizon, while farmers in the east grow corn, the state's best-known and most important crop. Ranching is also profitable in Nebraska, which ranks third behind Texas and Kansas in beef cattle production.

Nearly all Nebraska lies on the Great Plains, which begin near the junction of the Loup and Platte rivers. (The eastern edge of the state belongs to the Dissected Till Plains.) The terrain, mostly featureless, rises from east to west, but so gradually that it seems flat. Only near the Colorado border does the land give way to the buttes and valleys characteristic of the High Plains. One notable exception are the Sand Hills of north-central Nebraska, the largest sand dune area in North America. The soil there is held in place by grasses that also provide excellent forage for cattle.

They call it Huskermania. The University of Nebraska football team, nicknamed the Cornhuskers, has sold out every one of its home games since November 3, 1962. During those games, Memorial Stadium in Lincoln, seating 72,700 people, becomes—all by itself—the third largest city in the state.

Nebraska's Ogallala Aquifer sits at the northern end of the High Plains Aquifer, the nation's largest underground reservoir. Water pumped from the Ogallala Aquifer allows Nebraska farmers to irrigate more than seven million acres (about 3 million ha), the most irrigated land in any state after California and Texas.

The surveyors who laid out Nebraska (and most of the Great Plains) used a strict rectangular grid system. Townships were built up from square 640-acre (259-hectare) "sections," with the basic unit of settlement being the quarter-section farm.

Interstate Highways | State Capital | Native American Reservations | National Parks and Refuges | Grasslands | Highest Point

0 — miles — 100
0 — kilometers — 161

North Dakota typically ranks second behind Kansas in wheat production, yet every few years a particularly good harvest can nudge the state into first place. The two principal varieties grown in North Dakota are hard red spring wheat, used for making bread dough, and durum, from which spaghetti is made.

CANADA

Bottineau
Turtle Mountain Reservation
Fort Berthold Reservation
SOURIS RIVER
Minot
Rugby
Grafton
Williston
MISSOURI R.
Devils Lake
Devils Lake Reservation
Grand Forks
MINNESOTA
Lake Sakakawea
SHEYENNE RIVER
RED RIVER
YELLOWSTONE R.
Theodore Roosevelt National Park
Hazen
Carrington
29
Beulah
JAMES RIVER
Valley City
Fargo
Dickinson
Bismarck
94
Jamestown
MONTANA
HEART RIVER
Mandan
Long Lake
MISSOURI R.
Standing Rock Reservation
Lake Traverse Reservation
Wahpeton
Bowman
Ellendale
29
BOIS DE SIOUX R.
LITTLE MISSOURI RIVER

SOUTH DAKOTA

DID YOU KNOW?

that the typical North Dakota farmer grows enough food each year to feed 129 people for a year (up from 26 people in 1960)?

360 miles (579 km)

ABOUT NORTH DAKOTA

NICKNAME: Peace Garden State
CAPITAL: Bismarck
STATEHOOD: November 2, 1889 (39th)
MOTTO: Liberty and union, now and forever, one and inseparable.

POPULATION: 634,448 (48th)
AREA: 70,704 sq. mi. (19th)
(183,044 sq km)
HIGHEST POINT: 3,506 ft. (White Butte)
LOWEST POINT: 750 ft. (Red River)

FLOWER: Wild prairie rose
TREE: American elm
BIRD: Western meadowlark
FISH: Northern pike

North Dakota

Many North Dakotans have a lively sense of humor about their state. They tell jokes like "You know you're a North Dakotan if you define *summer* as three months of bad sledding." The climate there can indeed be challenging: Far from the moderating influence of an ocean and without trees or hills for windbreaks, North Dakota experiences some of the continent's hottest and coldest temperatures, not to mention frequent dust storms and blizzards. The weather, combined with the state's small population and apparently endless prairie landscape, might make a less hardy people lonely. Yet North Dakotans pride themselves on their positive outlook and spirit of cooperation.

Most of the businesses in the state depend on agriculture. The rich soil supports an abundance of wheat as well as the largest barley, flax, pinto bean, and sunflower crops in the country. Farms tend to be large, nearly three times the national average, which is why North Dakotans live so far apart. The state's tiny manufacturing sector is generally confined to the larger cities, where most of the factories process food—the pasta-making plant in Fargo, for instance, and the sugar beet refineries in Grand Forks.

Fargo and Grand Forks are located in the extremely fertile Red River Valley on the eastern edge of the state. The next regions over are the Drift Prairie and then the Missouri Plateau, a hilly and stony part of the Great Plains that covers the entire western half of North Dakota.

Because so many North Dakotans live in isolated areas, less than half the population has access to a library. To meet this need, most county libraries have established bookmobile programs to service rural areas.

Ice Age glaciers carved North Dakota into a series of stepped plateaus. From the Red River Valley, once the bottom of a huge glacial lake, the land rises sharply to the Drift Prairie (which takes its name from the glacial debris called drift). A similar step separates the Drift Prairie from the Missouri Plateau.

North Dakota has plenty of prairie grass but not much shade. Of the fifty states, it has the lowest percentage of forested land, only about 1 percent. The few trees that do grow there are mostly found in the Turtle Mountains.

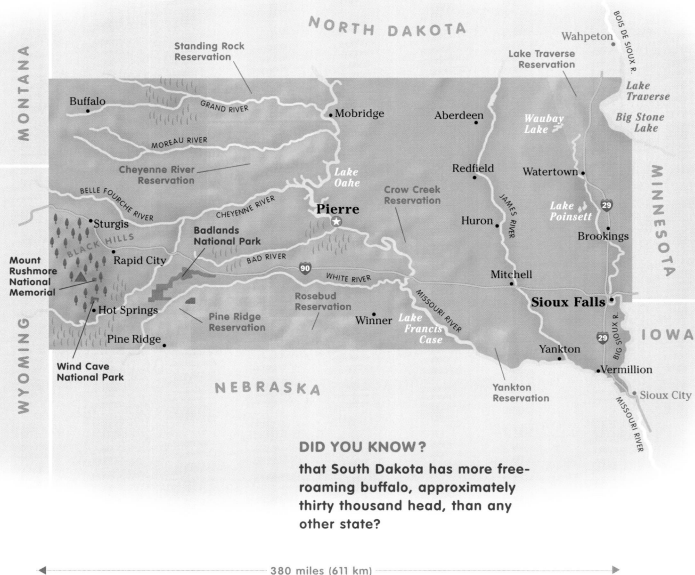

Interstate Highways **State Capital** **Native American Reservations** **National Forests** **National Parks and Refuges** **Grasslands** **Highest Point**

| 0 | miles | 100 |
| 0 | kilometers | 161 |

During the early 1980s, Citibank became the single largest employer in Sioux Falls when it moved its credit-card operations there. Since then, other financial services companies have followed, bringing more jobs and transforming Sioux Falls into an important center for credit-card processing.

DID YOU KNOW?

that South Dakota has more free-roaming buffalo, approximately thirty thousand head, than any other state?

380 miles (611 km)

ABOUT SOUTH DAKOTA

NICKNAME: Mount Rushmore State	**POPULATION:** 756,600 (46th)	**FLOWER:** Pasqueflower
CAPITAL: Pierre	**AREA:** 77,121 sq. mi. (17th)	**TREE:** Black Hills spruce
STATEHOOD: November 2, 1889 (40th)	(199,659 sq km)	**BIRD:** Ring-necked pheasant
MOTTO: Under God the people rule.	**HIGHEST POINT:** 7,242 ft. (Harney Peak)	**FISH:** Walleye
	LOWEST POINT: 966 ft. (Big Stone Lake)	

South Dakota

South Dakotans seem to live by two simple rules: Where the soil is fertile, you plant crops. Where the grass grows high, you raise livestock. In all, 91 percent of the land in the state is devoted to agriculture. In the fields of the east, farmers grow corn, wheat, hay, and other crops; in the grazing lands of the west, ranchers raise cattle, hogs, and sheep.

However, the Native Americans who live on South Dakota's many reservations are often unable to share in this agricultural prosperity. The reasons are mostly historical. For instance, the reservations onto which their ancestors were confined during the 1870s included some of the least arable land in the state. Nevertheless, many Sioux and Cheyenne leaders, while working hard to preserve ancient traditions, have helped their people find suitable modern lifestyles.

Winding among these reservations, the Missouri River is South Dakota's major geographical landmark. East of the river lies the Drift Prairie, where ancient glaciers left behind excellent farmland. Most South Dakotans live on this side of the river, on farms and in small towns. West of the Missouri, untouched by the glaciers that smoothed the eastern bank, are the dry, treeless grasslands of the Great Plains. Except for the area around the Black Hills, there are so few people in western South Dakota (an average of only three per square mile) that the land seems nearly deserted.

Native Americans, most of them Sioux, make up 8.3 percent of the South Dakota population. (Only Alaska and New Mexico have higher percentages.) Like many other nations, the Oglala Sioux, who live on the Pine Ridge Reservation, hold an annual powwow to celebrate their cultural heritage with craft displays and dancing competitions.

South Dakota has been so successful at promoting itself that tourism now ranks just behind agriculture in the state economy. One of the most popular sights is the quartet of presidential busts carved into the Black Hills at Mount Rushmore. Each head stands as tall as a six-story building.

Rising above southwestern South Dakota is a range of granite cliffs. The Sioux call this land Paha Sapa. Others call it the Black Hills because thick pine forests make the region look much darker than the surrounding plain.

CANADA

MISSOURI RIVER

Montana
page 96

YELLOWSTONE RIVER

Idaho
page 94

SNAKE RIVER

Wyoming
page 100

NORTH PLATTE RIVER

Utah
page 98

Colorado
page 92

SOUTH PLATTE RIVER

COLORADO RIVER

RIO GRANDE

ARKANSAS RIVER

MEXICO

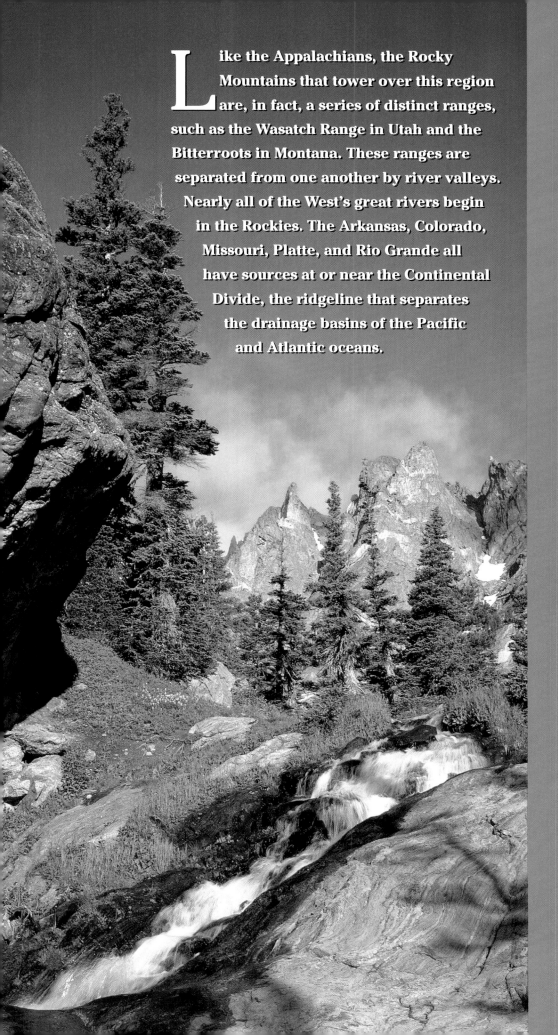

Like the Appalachians, the Rocky Mountains that tower over this region are, in fact, a series of distinct ranges, such as the Wasatch Range in Utah and the Bitterroots in Montana. These ranges are separated from one another by river valleys. Nearly all of the West's great rivers begin in the Rockies. The Arkansas, Colorado, Missouri, Platte, and Rio Grande all have sources at or near the Continental Divide, the ridgeline that separates the drainage basins of the Pacific and Atlantic oceans.

Mountain

Interstate Highways	State Capital	Native American Reservations	National Forests	National Parks and Refuges	Grasslands	Highest Point	miles	0 ... 100
							kilometers	0 ... 161

Colorado Springs, the home of the Air Force Academy, is the center of the state's robust defense and aerospace industries. Just south of town, for example, inside hollowed-out Cheyenne Mountain, the North American Aerospace Defense Command (NORAD) monitors U.S. and Canadian airspace for incoming aircraft and missiles.

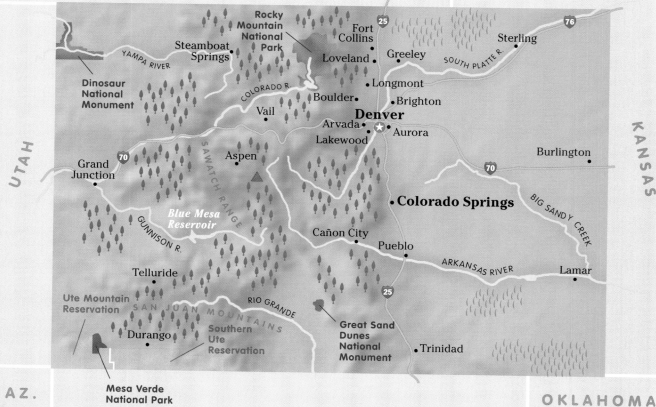

387 miles (623 km)

DID YOU KNOW?

that the lowest point in Colorado is higher than the highest point in eighteen states?

ABOUT COLORADO

NICKNAME: Centennial State
CAPITAL: Denver
STATEHOOD: August 1, 1876 (38th)
MOTTO: Nothing without providence.

POPULATION: 4,417,714 (24th)
AREA: 104,100 sq. mi. (8th)
(269,503 sq km)
HIGHEST POINT: 14,433 ft. (Mount Elbert)
LOWEST POINT: 3,350 ft. (Arkansas River)

FLOWER: Rocky Mountain columbine
TREE: Blue spruce
BIRD: Lark bunting

Colorado

More than in other states, the culture wars of the early twenty-first century are being fought in Colorado. On one side are the old-time, highly conservative, business-oriented Coloradans. On the other are environmentally conscious liberals, many of whom emigrated from California during the 1970s and 1980s. Lately, however, an influx of well-paid high-tech workers has shifted the political balance again, this time to the more conservative side, especially on such hot topics as the Rocky Mountains and whether they should be mined or protected.

The Rockies still support a profitable mining industry, and cattle ranches still cover the High Plains, yet the state's economy no longer depends so heavily on natural resources. Instead, as Colorado has become more multicultural, its economy has diversified as well, and light manufacturing—of scientific instruments, for example—has flourished. Colorado's recent economic boom has focused on the string of cities, from Pueblo north to Fort Collins, that line the eastern foothills of the Rockies. Most of the new money has concentrated here, as well as three quarters of the population.

Although Colorado is closely identified with the southern Rockies, much of the state happens to be flat. The eastern two-fifths belongs to the Great Plains, which rise gently from the Kansas border. The Rockies take up the central two-fifths, while the western fringe sits atop the Colorado Plateau. Wind and water have eroded this upland into a scenic maze of canyons and flat-topped hills called mesas.

Each winter, twelve million people visit Colorado's world-famous ski resorts. Among the most glamorous of these are Aspen and Vail. (Vail also happens to be the largest ski resort in North America.) Thanks to state-of-the-art snowmaking machines, the ski season begins as early as October and continues for eight months.

COLORADO IN CROSS SECTION

14,000 ft. / 4,267 m
12,000 ft. / 3,658 m
10,000 ft. / 3,048 m
8,000 ft. / 2,438 m
Mean Altitude: 6,800 ft. / 2,073 m
6,000 ft. / 1,829 m
4,000 ft. / 1,219 m
2,000 ft. / 610 m

Rocky Mountain High
Colorado's mean altitude of sixty-eight hundred feet is the highest of any state. Nationwide, there are ninety-one peaks above fourteen thousand feet. Of these ninety-one "fourteeners," fifty-six are in Colorado.

With Colorado's growth, Denver has become the transportation and financial center of the Mountain West. It's called the Mile High City because it sits at an average elevation of 5,280 feet (1,609 m).

93

LEGEND

Interstate Highways   State Capital   Native American Reservations   National Forests   National Parks and Refuges   Highest Point

0   miles   100
0   kilometers   161

CANADA

WASH.

Priest Lake

Sandpoint

Lake Pend Oreille

Spokane

Coeur d'Alene

Kellog

90

Coeur d'Alene Reservation

CLEARWATER RIVER

Moscow

Missoula

Nez Perce Reservation

Lewiston

SELWAY RIVER

S. FORK CLEARWATER R.

DID YOU KNOW?

that the wiggle in Idaho's otherwise straight western border is Hells Canyon, the continent's deepest river-carved gorge?

Grangeville

CLEARWATER MTS.

SALMON RIVER

MONTANA

Butte

SNAKE RIVER

SALMON RIVER MTS.

Salmon

SAWTOOTH MTS.

Clear Springs Foods, headquartered near Twin Falls, is the world's leading producer of aqua-cultured rainbow trout. Altogether, companies in south-central Idaho produce about 75 percent of the food-size trout sold in the United States. The fish are raised in ponds cooled by underground springs.

Yellowstone National Park

15

Sun Valley

Ketchum

Hailey

Craters of the Moon National Monument

Rexburg

Idaho Falls

Caldwell

★ **Boise**

Nampa

Mountain Home

SNAKE RIVER PLAIN

Grays Lake

WYO.

84

Duck Valley Reservation

American Falls Reservoir

86

Pocatello

Fort Hall Reservation

15

Twin Falls

Burley

84

Preston

Bear Lake

OREGON

NEVADA

UTAH

Logan

← 305 miles (491 km) →

ABOUT IDAHO

NICKNAME: Gem State
CAPITAL: Boise
STATEHOOD: July 3, 1890 (43rd)
MOTTO: Let it be perpetual.

POPULATION: 1,321,006 (39th)
AREA: 83,574 sq. mi. (14th)
(216,363 sq km)
HIGHEST POINT: 12,662 ft. (Borah Peak)
LOWEST POINT: 710 ft. (Snake River)

FLOWER: Syringa
TREE: Western white pine
BIRD: Mountain bluebird
FISH: Cutthroat trout

Idaho

The Idaho Potato Commission spends bushels and bushels of money each year to make certain that the words *Idaho* and *potato* remain closely linked in the American mind. In return, the Idaho potato industry generates $2.5 billion a year, or 15 percent of the state's gross product, which is no small potatoes.

Yet to dismiss Idaho as a single giant potato farm would be wrong. For one thing, the many potato farms there are crowded into just one small section of the state, the Snake River Plain, which is Idaho's only level ground. Elsewhere, the state is a wilderness of forests and mountains, including some of the country's most rugged and least accessible land. Residents of the Idaho Panhandle, in particular, tend to be independent and self-reliant, because they have no other choice.

Although Idaho, like most mountain states, has some mineral and timber resources, environmentally conscious residents are much more interested in developing the state's wilderness tourism industry. For example, thanks to federal protection, the Salmon and Clearwater rivers have both become meccas for white-water rafters.

Except for isolated timber and mining settlements, most towns in Idaho follow the course of the Snake River, and most people live on the Snake River Plain atop the Columbia Plateau. Aside from a lip of the Great Basin jutting into the state from Utah, the rest of Idaho—specifically, the northern two-thirds—belongs to the Rocky Mountains.

At the World Center for Birds of Prey in Boise, the Peregrine Fund houses over two hundred endangered hunting birds, including California condors, harpy eagles, and Aplomado falcons. An international leader in endangered species research, the center breeds these birds in captivity, then releases their young into the wild.

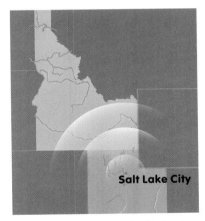

Salt Lake City

After Utah, Idaho has the highest concentration of Mormons, or members of the Church of Jesus Christ of Latter-day Saints. Statewide, Mormons make up about 27 percent of the population. However, near the Utah border in Idaho's desert southeast, many towns are as much as 90 percent Mormon.

Idaho boasts eighteen million acres (about 7 million ha) of wilderness, the most of any state after Alaska. In fact, some parts of the mountainous, heavily forested Panhandle have remained essentially unchanged since Lewis and Clark explored them in 1805.

LEGEND

🛣️ **20** Interstate Highways	✪ State Capital	⬜ Native American Reservations	🌲 National Forests	⬛ National Parks and Refuges	▲ Highest Point	0 — miles — 100 0 — kilometers — 161

Nearly all the manufacturing in Montana makes use of the state's natural resources. For example, lumber and wood products such as pencils and telephone poles account for about one third of the state's total output. The rest are mostly oil, coal, metal, and food products.

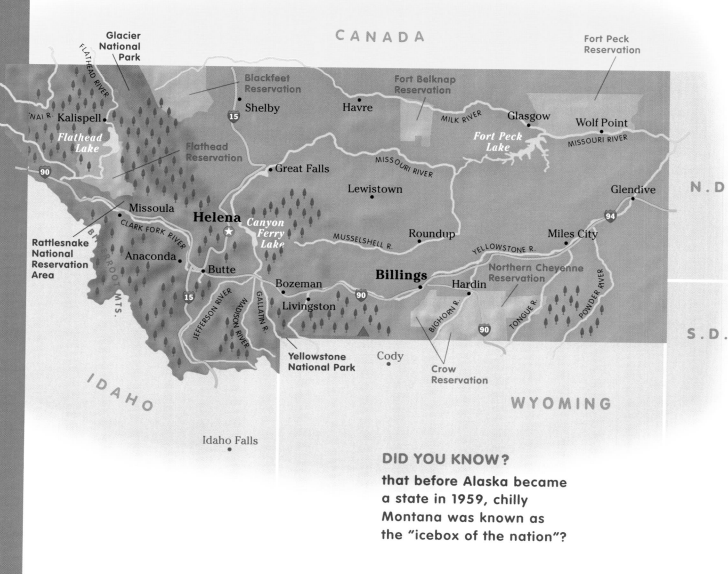

CANADA

Glacier National Park

Blackfeet Reservation

Fort Belknap Reservation

Fort Peck Reservation

FLATHEAD RIVER

Shelby

Havre

MILK RIVER

Glasgow

Wolf Point

KOOTENAI R.

Kalispell

15

Flathead Lake

Flathead Reservation

Fort Peck Lake

MISSOURI RIVER

90

Great Falls

MISSOURI RIVER

Lewistown

Glendive

N. D.

Missoula

Helena ☆

Canyon Ferry Lake

CLARK FORK RIVER

MUSSELSHELL R.

Roundup

Miles City

94

Rattlesnake National Reservation Area

BITTERROOT MTS.

Anaconda

Butte

15

Bozeman

Billings

Hardin

YELLOWSTONE R.

Northern Cheyenne Reservation

POWDER RIVER

S. D.

JEFFERSON RIVER

MADISON RIVER

GALLATIN R.

Livingston

90

BIGHORN R.

TONGUE R.

IDAHO

Yellowstone National Park

Cody

Crow Reservation

90

WYOMING

Idaho Falls

DID YOU KNOW?

that before Alaska became a state in 1959, chilly Montana was known as the "icebox of the nation"?

◄------------- 570 miles (917 km) -------------►

ABOUT MONTANA

NICKNAME: Treasure State
CAPITAL: Helena
STATEHOOD: November 8, 1889 (41st)
MOTTO: Gold and silver.

POPULATION: 904,433 (44th)
AREA: 147,046 sq. mi. (4th)
(380,685 sq km)
HIGHEST POINT: 12,799 ft. (Granite Peak)
LOWEST POINT: 1,800 ft. (Kootenai River)

FLOWER: Bitterroot
TREE: Ponderosa pine
BIRD: Western meadowlark
FISH: Cutthroat trout

Montana

There are so few Montanans that parts of the state, the fourth largest, seem uninhabited. Attracted by this solitude, more and more celebrities have been buying ranches there to get away from it all. Meanwhile, the people who live there don't seem to take much notice. They're mostly cattle ranchers and wheat farmers, though a good number work for mining companies. The state's gold, silver, and copper supplies have largely run out, but oil, coal, and natural gas have taken their place.

As oil drilling and coal mining have expanded, they've become more controversial, especially among Montana's Native Americans. (The largest group after whites, they make up 6 percent of the state's population.) Most Native Americans living on Montana reservations urgently need the jobs and income mining would provide. However, many reservation leaders worry that exploiting these resources might permanently damage the environment.

Montana is called Big Sky Country because in the eastern two-thirds of the state, where the land is flat and open, it's easy to see a lot of sky. Buttes and small mountain ranges occasionally interrupt this treeless Great Plains grassland, but they seem insignificant compared with the Rocky Mountains of western Montana, along whose backbone runs the Continental Divide. In general, rain that falls on the western side of this divide runs into the Pacific Ocean, while rain that falls on its eastern side drains into the Atlantic.

Life in Montana is strongly oriented toward the outdoors. One reason is that the hunting and fishing there are exceptional: The Yellowstone River, for example, offers some of the best fly-fishing in the world.

Chinook Winds

Chinooks are unusually warm, dry winds that blow down from the Rockies every so often during winter. They can raise the air temperature 40°F (22°C) in less than an hour and melt enough snow so that cattle can graze—at least until the next snowfall.

Western Montana includes some of the most difficult and out-of-the-way territory in the country. There are mountains in Glacier National Park so steep and remote that no one has ever climbed them.

LEGEND

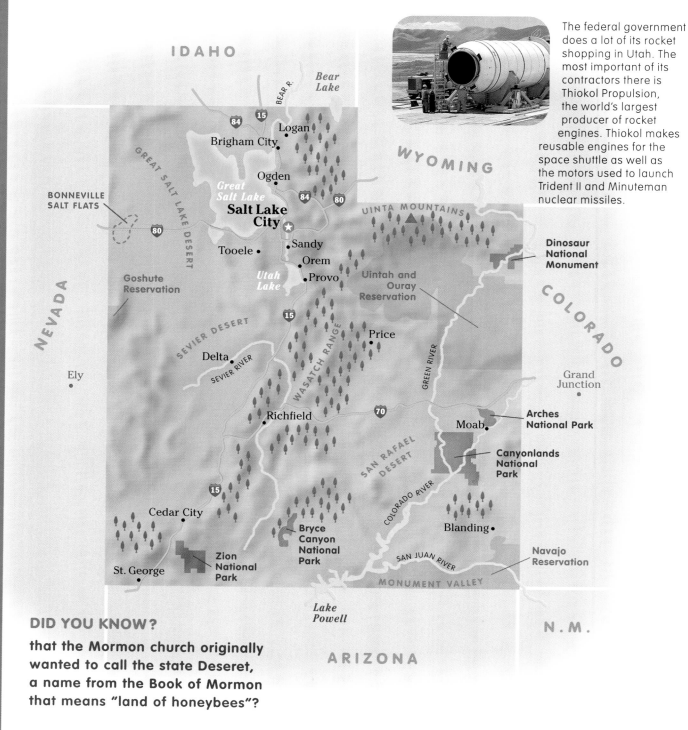

Interstate Highways

State Capital

Native American Reservations

National Forests

National Parks and Refuges

Highest Point

| 0 | miles | 100 |
| 0 | kilometers | 161 |

IDAHO

Bear R.

Bear Lake

84 · 15

Logan

Brigham City

Ogden

Great Salt Lake

GREAT SALT LAKE DESERT

BONNEVILLE SALT FLATS

80

Salt Lake City ★

Tooele ·

Sandy ·

Orem ·

· Provo

Utah Lake

Goshute Reservation

NEVADA

Ely ·

SEVIER DESERT

Delta ·

SEVIER RIVER

15

Richfield ·

Cedar City ·

15

St. George ·

Zion National Park

Bryce Canyon National Park

Lake Powell

ARIZONA

WYOMING

UINTA MOUNTAINS ▲

Uintah and Ouray Reservation

WASATCH RANGE

· Price

GREEN RIVER

70

SAN RAFAEL DESERT

Moab ·

COLORADO RIVER

· Blanding

SAN JUAN RIVER

MONUMENT VALLEY

Navajo Reservation

Dinosaur National Monument

COLORADO

Grand Junction ·

Arches National Park

Canyonlands National Park

N.M.

The federal government does a lot of its rocket shopping in Utah. The most important of its contractors there is Thiokol Propulsion, the world's largest producer of rocket engines. Thiokol makes reusable engines for the space shuttle as well as the motors used to launch Trident II and Minuteman nuclear missiles.

DID YOU KNOW?

that the Mormon church originally wanted to call the state Deseret, a name from the Book of Mormon that means "land of honeybees"?

◄———— 275 miles (442 km) ————►

ABOUT UTAH

NICKNAME: Beehive State
CAPITAL: Salt Lake City
STATEHOOD: January 4, 1896 (45th)
MOTTO: Industry.

POPULATION: 2,269,789 (34th)
AREA: 84,904 sq. mi. (13th) (219,806 sq km)
HIGHEST POINT: 13,528 ft. (Kings Peak)
LOWEST POINT: 2,000 ft. (Beaverdam Wash)

FLOWER: Sego lily
TREE: Blue spruce
BIRD: California seagull
FISH: Bonneville cutthroat trout

Utah

The U.S. Constitution demands a separation between church and state. Yet it's difficult to imagine Utah without the Mormon church, also known as the Church of Jesus Christ of Latter-day Saints. A group of Mormons led by Brigham Young settled Utah in 1847, and Mormons still make up 70 percent of the population. Although the Mormon church no longer governs the state, it continues to play an important role in Utah's social life and institutions. For example, the Mormon preference for large families has kept the Utah birthrate well above the national average.

The Mormons were allowed to claim Utah, the nation's second driest state (after Nevada), largely because no other settlers wanted it. Most of the land, though geologically spectacular, cannot be farmed. What little arable land there is sits in a narrow band at the foot of the Wasatch Mountains, where streams fed by snowmelt carry water and mineral sediments down from the Rockies. As a result, about 80 percent of the population lives along the Wasatch Front between Provo and Ogden.

In the Rockies, the biggest business is mining, primarily gold, silver, and lead. To the south and east, the mountains flatten out into the Colorado Plateau, which covers slightly more than half the state. In this scenic region, featuring Zion and Bryce Canyon national parks, tourism is the most important industry. The western third of Utah belongs to the Great Basin and contains the Sevier and Great Salt Lake deserts as well as some of the flattest land on the continent.

Among Christians, Mormons are remarkable for having many beliefs uniquely their own, including their emphasis on business. To finance extensive missionary activities, the Mormon church runs many for-profit companies, including a department-store chain, an insurance company, and a "citrus ranch" in Florida.

The Great Salt Lake is all that's left of a huge freshwater lake that once covered western Utah. This ancient body of water, Lake Bonneville, was about the size that Lake Michigan is today. However, when the surrounding land rose, Lake Bonneville dried up, leaving the Great Salt Lake behind.

Southern Utah boasts some of the most spectacular rock formations on the North American continent. The buttes of Monument Valley may look familiar because they've appeared in many classic Hollywood westerns.

LEGEND

Interstate Highways   State Capital   Native American Reservations   National Forests   National Parks and Refuges   Grasslands   Highest Point

	miles	100
0	kilometers	161
0		

Oil is the most valuable mineral in Wyoming, which produces about ninety million barrels of crude each year. This amount ranks the state fourth nationally behind Texas, Louisiana, and California. Many economists believe that Wyoming's future will depend increasingly on mining—particularly its reserves of oil, coal, and natural gas.

DID YOU KNOW?

that the 308-foot (94-meter) Lower Falls of the Yellowstone River is twice the height of Niagara Falls?

365 miles (587 km)

ABOUT WYOMING

NICKNAME: Equality State

CAPITAL: Cheyenne

STATEHOOD: July 10, 1890 (44th)

MOTTO: Equal rights.

POPULATION: 494,423 (50th)

AREA: 97,818 sq. mi. (10th)
(253,239 sq km)

HIGHEST POINT: 13,804 ft. (Gannett Peak)

LOWEST POINT: 3,099 ft. (Belle Fourche River)

FLOWER: Indian paintbrush

TREE: Plains cottonwood

BIRD: Meadowlark

FISH: Cutthroat trout

Wyoming

Famous for its scenic beauty, Wyoming attracts nearly five million tourists a year. Many come to visit Yellowstone and Grand Teton national parks, yet few stay. The population of Wyoming, despite its large size, is the lowest of any state in the Union, perhaps because life on its dry plains and in its rugged mountains can be so difficult.

Most of the people who live in Wyoming are the descendants of the whites, Mexicans, and Native Americans who originally settled the land. The state's many ranches and rodeos give the impression that Wyoming is the last refuge of the American cowboy. In fact, many Wyoming ranchers have to hire cowboys from Mexico, Chile, and Peru to do this hard, lonesome work.

Ranching and other farming activities generate $900 million a year for Wyoming, yet agriculture ranks a distant third in the state economy. Mining is far and away Wyoming's biggest business, at $4.7 billion per year (with tourism second). In addition to its plentiful oil, Wyoming has huge coal reserves, the nation's largest, enough to last more than three hundred years.

Only the eastern fringe of Wyoming lies on the Great Plains. The rest of the state, which straddles the Continental Divide, belongs to the Rocky Mountains. Separating Wyoming's many ranges are the dry flatlands of the Intermontane Basin. Much of Wyoming's mineral wealth rests beneath these high, cold plateaus, whose short-grass prairies provide excellent grazing for the state's largest cattle ranches.

Cheyenne began hosting its annual Frontier Days celebration in 1897. The rodeo was the brainchild of a Union Pacific railroad agent who wanted to promote his trains but needed a destination. Today, more than twelve hundred cowboys and cowgirls take part in the roping, riding, and steer-wrestling competitions.

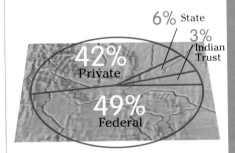

6% State
3% Indian Trust
42% Private
49% Federal

The federal government still owns a great deal of land in the West. For example, it owns 49 percent of Wyoming and more than half of western Montana.

Compared to the size of its human population, Wyoming's cattle and sheep populations are huge. Furthermore, rangeland there covers a whopping 88 percent of the farmland.

101

CANADA

COLORADO RIVER

ARKANSAS RIVER

RED RIVER

RIO GRANDE

PACIFIC OCEAN

MEXICO

GULF OF MEXICO

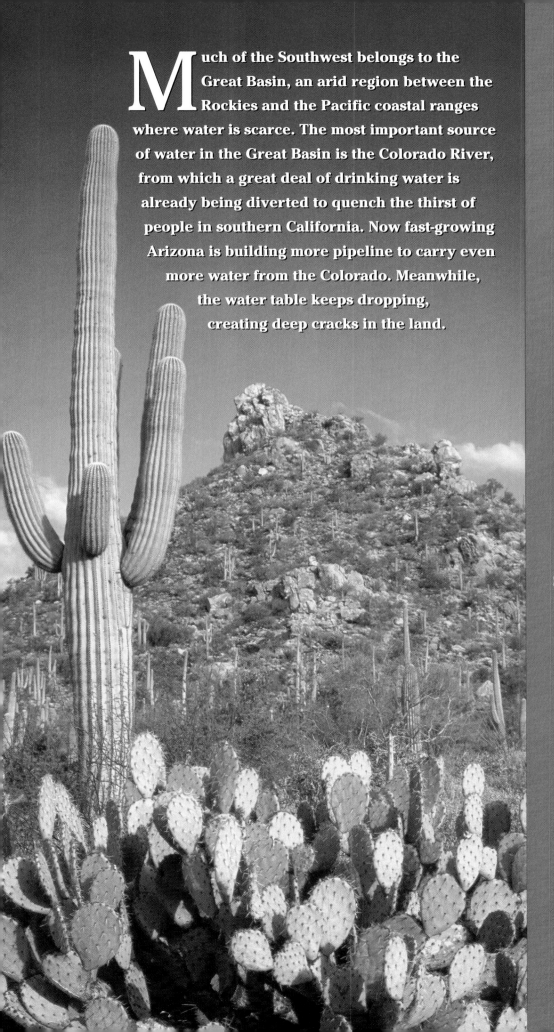

Much of the Southwest belongs to the Great Basin, an arid region between the Rockies and the Pacific coastal ranges where water is scarce. The most important source of water in the Great Basin is the Colorado River, from which a great deal of drinking water is already being diverted to quench the thirst of people in southern California. Now fast-growing Arizona is building more pipeline to carry even more water from the Colorado. Meanwhile, the water table keeps dropping, creating deep cracks in the land.

Southwest

LEGEND

🛣️ **20** Interstate Highways

⭐ **State Capital**

🟩 **Native American Reservations**

🌲 **National Forests**

🟥 **National Parks and Refuges**

🔺 **Highest Point**

0 — miles — 100
0 — kilometers — 161

DID YOU KNOW?

that the Grand Canyon is more than one mile (1.6 km) deep in some places and as many as eighteen miles (29 km) wide?

UTAH

COLO.

NEVADA

St. George

Lake Powell

15

Grand Canyon National Park

3

Canyon de Chelly National Monument

Las Vegas

Lake Mead

2

COLORADO R.

1

PAINTED DESERT

4

LITTLE COLORADO R.

Window Rock

Gallup

CALIFORNIA

Bullhead City

Kingman

40

Flagstaff

Winslow

40

Holbrook

Petrified Forest National Park

Lake Havasu City

Prescott

VERDE R.

MOGOLLON RIM

Lake Havasu

17

Theodore Roosevelt Lake

SALT RIVER

5

NEW MEXICO

9

10

Glendale

Scottsdale

Phoenix ⭐ • Mesa

6

Tempe

Chandler

7 **10**

Casa Grande

Clifton

SONORAN DESERT

GILA RIVER

8

Safford

Yuma

Organ Pipe Cactus National Monument

10

Tucson

10

8

Arizona produces more nonfuel minerals than any other state except Nevada. Its open-pit copper mines, for example, supply two thirds of the annual U.S. output of copper. Arizona's mines also yield gold, silver, and gemstones, but copper dominates, accounting for more than 85 percent of the state's nonfuel mineral income.

19

Sierra Vista

Nogales

Douglas

Gulf of California

MEXICO

NATIVE AMERICAN RESERVATIONS

① Hualapal
② Havasupal
③ Navajo
④ Hopi
⑤ Fort Apache
⑥ San Carlos
⑦ Gila River
⑧ Tohono O'Odham
⑨ Colorado River

← 340 miles (547 km) →

ABOUT ARIZONA

NICKNAME: Grand Canyon State

CAPITAL: Phoenix

STATEHOOD: February 14, 1912 (48th)

MOTTO: God enriches.

POPULATION: 5,307,331 (20th)

AREA: 114,006 sq. mi. (6th)
(295,148 sq km)

HIGHEST POINT: 12,633 ft. (Humphreys Peak)

LOWEST POINT: 70 ft. (Colorado River)

FLOWER: Saguaro

TREE: Paloverde

BIRD: Cactus wren

FISH: Apache trout

Arizona

Arizona has always been known for its clean air and abundant sunshine. Yet until the 1960s, life in this desert state appealed mostly to people with breathing problems because the heat was so intense. With the advent of affordable air conditioning, however, many retired Americans also began to take advantage of the region's climate. Now, with manufacturing and construction jobs booming there, people of all ages are flocking to Arizona, which trails only Nevada as the nation's fastest-growing state.

Most of these newcomers have settled in the sprawling suburbs of Phoenix and Tucson, where four out of every five Arizonans live. However, the arrival of all these people has threatened—ironically—the very qualities of life that initially attracted them (and so many others) to the Sun Belt. More cars mean dirtier air, more new homes mean less natural scenery, and more people in general mean a greater strain on the state's natural resources, especially its water.

Arizona's most important source of water is the Colorado River, running through the 277-mile-long (446-kilometer -long) Grand Canyon. The canyon sits on the western edge of the scenic Colorado Plateau— a dry, high tableland cut by deep gorges and studded with mesas. A line of cliffs called the Mogollon Rim separates the Colorado Plateau from the Basin and Range system that covers southern and western Arizona. The "basins" of this system are the arid plains of the Sonoran Desert from which mountain "ranges" such as the Chiricahua rise occasionally, like islands from the sea.

Although no longer a part of Mexico, Arizona continues to maintain strong ties to its southern neighbor. Because one in four Arizonans is Hispanic, Mexican influences abound. Mexican architecture, home furnishings, clothing, music, and food have all become important parts of the Arizona lifestyle.

The Sonoran Desert contains many unique plants and animals. The most famous of these is the saguaro cactus, which can grow fifty feet (15 m) tall and live for more than one hundred years.

Mapmakers use dots and dashes to show rivers that dry up during part of the year. There are many such intermittent rivers in Arizona. Stretches of the Little Colorado, for example, flow only during winter and spring, when rains and melting snow provide sufficient water.

20 Interstate Highways | ★ State Capital | Native American Reservations | National Forests | National Parks and Refuges | ▲ Highest Point

0 miles 100
0 kilometers 161

DID YOU KNOW?

that Nevada, with no waiting periods and many drive-through chapels, leads the nation in weddings with ten times the national average?

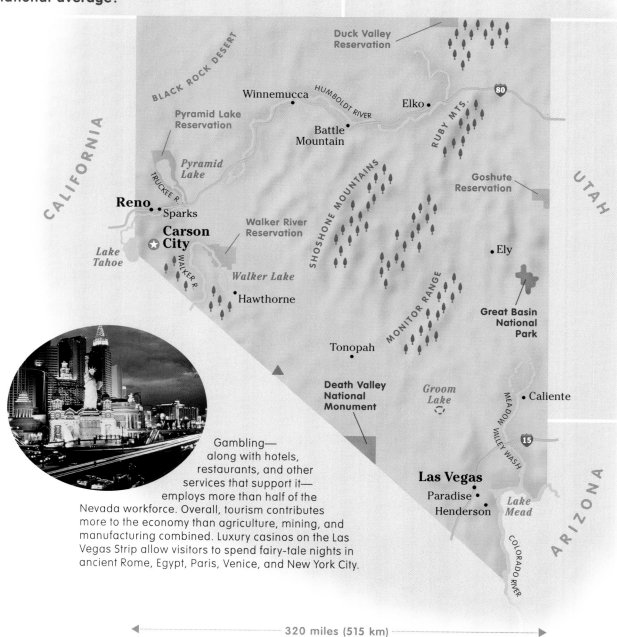

OREGON

IDAHO

Duck Valley Reservation

BLACK ROCK DESERT

Winnemucca

HUMBOLDT RIVER

Elko

80

Pyramid Lake Reservation

Battle Mountain

RUBY MTS.

CALIFORNIA

Pyramid Lake

TRUCKEE R.

SHOSHONE MOUNTAINS

Goshute Reservation

UTAH

Reno • Sparks

Walker River Reservation

Carson City ★

WALKER R.

• Ely

Lake Tahoe

Walker Lake

MONITOR RANGE

Great Basin National Park

• Hawthorne

Tonopah

▲

Death Valley National Monument

Groom Lake

• Caliente

MEADOW VALLEY WASH

15

ARIZONA

Las Vegas
Paradise •
Henderson

Lake Mead

COLORADO RIVER

Gambling— along with hotels, restaurants, and other services that support it— employs more than half of the Nevada workforce. Overall, tourism contributes more to the economy than agriculture, mining, and manufacturing combined. Luxury casinos on the Las Vegas Strip allow visitors to spend fairy-tale nights in ancient Rome, Egypt, Paris, Venice, and New York City.

320 miles (515 km)

ABOUT NEVADA

NICKNAME: Silver State
CAPITAL: Carson City
STATEHOOD: October 31, 1864 (36th)
MOTTO: All for our country.

POPULATION: 2,106,074 (35th)
AREA: 110,567 sq. mi. (7th)
(286,245 sq km)
HIGHEST POINT: 13,140 ft. (Boundary Peak)
LOWEST POINT: 479 ft. (Colorado River)

FLOWER: Sagebrush
TREE: Single-leaf piñon, bristlecone pine
BIRD: Mountain bluebird
FISH: Lahontan cutthroat trout

Nevada

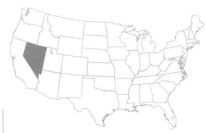

Because of its excessively dry climate and barren landscape, Nevada was one of the last U.S. territories to be explored and settled. Nineteenth-century gold and silver strikes lured prospectors—and Nevada still leads the nation in gold and silver mining—but those prospectors didn't stay long. During the Great Depression, Nevada attracted some attention with laws that made marriage and divorce much easier, yet it was legalized gambling, enacted in 1931, that assured the state's future prosperity.

Although Nevada retains many rugged frontier qualities, casino money has transformed both Las Vegas and Reno into sophisticated metropolitan areas housing more than 80 percent of the state's population. With the exception of the southern desert, the rest of the state belongs to what residents call the "cow counties," where cattle and sheep graze on leased public land before being shipped to California or the Midwest for fattening. The lack of water, of course, limits most other types of agriculture.

In fact, with just nine inches (23 cm) of precipitation per year, Nevada is the driest state. Except for a small spur of the Sierra Nevada near Lake Tahoe, most of Nevada belongs to the arid Great Basin. The water that makes Las Vegas possible comes primarily from Lake Mead, the largest U.S. reservoir, which stretches for 115 miles (185 km) behind the Hoover Dam on the Colorado River.

Nevada's clear skies and open desert terrain provide ideal conditions for testing military aircraft. Over the years, many mysterious planes have been tested at Area 51, a top-secret air force base near Groom Lake. Often these planes are mistaken for UFOs. As a result, Route 375, which runs past Groom Lake, has been nick-named the Extraterrestrial Highway.

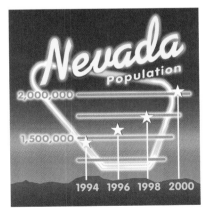

Nevada is the nation's fastest-growing state. Since 1980, its population has more than doubled. Nearly all that growth has come within existing metropolitan areas, especially the suburbs of Las Vegas.

Although Nevada averages nine inches (23 cm) of precipitation per year statewide, less than four inches (10 cm) of rain falls on the parched southern Nevada desert, where Death Valley National Monument is located.

LEGEND

Interstate Highways	State Capital	Native American Reservations	National Forests	National Parks and Refuges	Highest Point	0 miles 100	0 kilometers 161	

Since the 1940s, the Los Alamos National Laboratory has made New Mexico a center for scientific research. Los Alamos and other federal facilities, including the Sandia National Laboratories in Albuquerque, attract highly educated workers, often from outside the state.

UTAH COLORADO OKLA.

DID YOU KNOW?

that at Four Corners on the Navajo Reservation you can lie down in four states at the same time?

Durango

① Farmington
SAN JUAN RIVER
②
㉒
Raton
Taos ③
Los Alamos ④ ⑤ ⑥ ⑦
⑧
⑨
Gallup
⑨
⑩ ⑫
⑩ ⑪ **Santa Fe** Las Vegas
⑬
⑭ **Rio Rancho**
⑮ **Albuquerque**
⑳ ⑲ ⑰ ⑭
⑯
⑭

Conchas Lake
CANADIAN R.
Tucumcari

RIO PUERCO
RIO GRANDE

ARIZONA

TEXAS

Clovis
Portales

Socorro

GILA RIVER

Elephant Butte Reservoir

Truth or Consequences

Silver City

Las Cruces
Deming
El Paso

⑩

⑩

PECOS RIVER

Roswell

⑱

㉑ Alamogordo

White Sands National Monument

Hobbs

Carlsbad

Carlsbad Caverns National Park

SANGRE DE CRISTO MTS.

25
40
40
25

MAJOR NATIVE AMERICAN RESERVATIONS

① Ute Mountain
② Jicarilla Apache
③ Taos
④ Santa Clara
⑤ San Ildefonso
⑥ Pojoaque
⑦ Nambe
⑧ Tesuque
⑨ Jemez
⑩ Zia
⑪ Santa Ana
⑫ Santo Domingo
⑬ San Filipe
⑭ Laguna
⑮ Cañoncito
⑯ Isleta
⑰ Acoma
⑱ Alamo Navajo
⑲ Ramah Navajo
⑳ Zuni
㉑ Mescalero
㉒ Navajo

MEXICO

◄—————— 352 miles (566 km) ——————►

ABOUT NEW MEXICO

NICKNAME: Land of Enchantment
CAPITAL: Santa Fe
STATEHOOD: January 6, 1912 (47th)
MOTTO: It grows as it goes.

POPULATION: 1,829,146 (36th)
AREA: 121,598 sq. mi. (5th)
(314,803 sq km)
HIGHEST POINT: 13,161 ft. (Wheeler Peak)
LOWEST POINT: 2,842 ft. (Red Bluff Reservoir)

FLOWER: Yucca
TREE: Piñon
BIRD: Roadrunner
FISH: Rio Grande cutthroat trout

New Mexico

For many years, New Mexico has attracted top artists from all over the world. Painters, notably Georgia O'Keeffe, came to record the state's unique physical beauty. Writers, on the other hand, have generally been more interested in observing New Mexico's extraordinary cultural diversity. With a population that's 42 percent Hispanic (the highest percentage of any state) and 9 percent Native American (the second highest percentage), New Mexico is an ongoing experiment. The purpose of this experiment? To find out how people of radically different backgrounds can live together while still maintaining their separate cultural identities.

Although art galleries have prospered in Santa Fe and Taos, most New Mexicans depend on farming, ranching, and mining for their livelihoods. New Mexico, for example, ranks third in copper production, sixth in uranium, and enjoys large reserves of oil, coal, and natural gas. In 1999, despite some local opposition, the nation's first permanent nuclear waste disposal site opened in the desert east of Carlsbad, accepting radioactive waste from Los Alamos and other nuclear weapons laboratories.

New Mexico's eastern third, a part of the Great Plains, is often called Little Texas because its cattle ranches, oil fields, and military bases remind people of the state next door. Farther west, the fertile Rio Grande Valley runs through the southern Rockies. The rest of the state belongs to the high Colorado Plateau in the northwest and a Basin and Range system in the south.

The Navajo of New Mexico are famous for their blankets, the Zuni for their turquoise-and-silver jewelry, and the Pueblo for their pots. Pueblo pottery is typically painted with geometric designs that identify the potter's village.

Humorist Will Rogers once called the enormous Carlsbad Caverns "the Grand Canyon with a roof on it." From late spring through fall, three hundred thousand Mexican free-tailed bats depart nightly at dusk to hunt for insects. People have compared this swarm to a column of smoke rising from the cave entrance.

From the desert basins of southern New Mexico, the land rises steadily as one moves north, climbing ten thousand feet (3,000 m) to the snowy Sangre de Cristo Mountains north of Taos.

LEGEND

20 Interstate Highways	⊛ State Capital	Native American Reservations	National Forests	National Parks and Refuges	Grasslands	▲ Highest Point	0 ⊢⊣ 0	miles kilometers	100 161

Pump It Up

Wells are a familiar sight in Oklahoma. In fact, eighteen wells once pumped oil from beneath the grounds of the state capitol. Although nearly every county in Oklahoma has oil and natural gas, the most important fields are found near Tulsa, the center of the state's petroleum industry.

KANSAS

Wichita

Salt Plains National Wildlife Refuge

Osage Reservation

MISSOURI

SALT FORK RIVER

Alva

Great Salt Plains Lake

Ponca City

Bartlesville

Miami

COL.

N.M.

▲

Guymon

Optima Lake

Woodward

CIMARRON RIVER

Enid

Lake of the Cherokees

Canton Lake

Stillwater

Tulsa

Broken Arrow

CANADIAN R.

DID YOU KNOW?

that Oklahoma averages fifty tornadoes a year, with the most coming in April and May?

Edmond

Midwest City

Muskogee

ARKANSAS R.

Fort Smith

Elk City

40

Oklahoma City

Shawnee

Eufaula Lake

Robert S. Kerr Lake

Anadarko

Norman

Ada

McAlester

WICHITA MTS.

WASHITA RIVER

OUACHITA MTS.

Altus

Lawton

Duncan

35

Broken Bow Lake

ARKANSAS

44

RED RIVER

Ardmore

Lake Texoma

Idabel

TEXAS

Fort Worth

Dallas

◄———————— 464 miles (747 km) ————————►

ABOUT OKLAHOMA

NICKNAME: Sooner State

CAPITAL: Oklahoma City

STATEHOOD: November 16, 1907 (46th)

MOTTO: Labor conquers all.

POPULATION: 3,460,097 (28th)

AREA: 69,903 sq. mi. (20th) (180,971 sq km)

HIGHEST POINT: 4,973 ft. (Black Mesa)

LOWEST POINT: 289 ft. (Little River)

FLOWER: Mistletoe

TREE: Redbud

BIRD: Scissor-tailed flycatcher

FISH: White bass

Oklahoma

The people who live along the Red River in southern Oklahoma call their region Little Dixie because it reminds them of the Deep South, where their great-great-grandfathers farmed before moving west. Similarly, the wheat fields of northern Oklahoma show the influence of the transplanted Kansans who first tilled the soil there. However, from the Ouachita Mountains to the Panhandle, the rest of Oklahoma is truly cowboy country, and the state prides itself on its colorful western heritage.

For a long time, both the cowboys and the Native Americans in Oklahoma struggled. During the nineteenth century, Oklahoma was called the Indian Territory because the federal government had relocated so many Native Americans there. The terrain was so barren that no one thought whites would ever want to live there. Even during the twentieth century, the prolonged drought of the Dust Bowl years forced hundreds of thousands of Oklahomans to leave the state.

Yet today the descendants of Oklahoma's cowboys and Native Americans are flourishing. Improved soil conservation has reclaimed so much farmland that Oklahoma currently ranks fourth in wheat production. It also ranks third in beef cattle, the state's leading agricultural product. Even bigger money comes from oil and natural gas.

Overall, Oklahoma is a jumble of environments: The northeastern corner, for example, sits on the edge of the hilly, cool Ozark Plateau. The High Plains climate on the Panhandle, however, is much hotter and drier.

After California, Oklahoma has more Native American residents than any other state—about 270,000, or 7.9 percent of the population. Yet there are few reservations in Oklahoma because the Cherokee and other Native American nations have become so well integrated. In 1985, for example, the Cherokee Nation took the nontraditional step of electing its first female chief, Wilma Mankiller (pictured above).

Oklahoma has extremely varied microclimates because it occupies two weather transition zones: from north to south as well as from east to west. At any given time, cool northern, warm southern, dry western, or humid eastern air may dominate. However, when two or more of these air masses meet, the result can be a blizzard, a thunderstorm, or even a tornado.

The humid Red River Valley defines Oklahoma's southern border with Texas. The farmers there grow cotton, peanuts, and other crops that immigrants from the South brought with them during the nineteenth century.

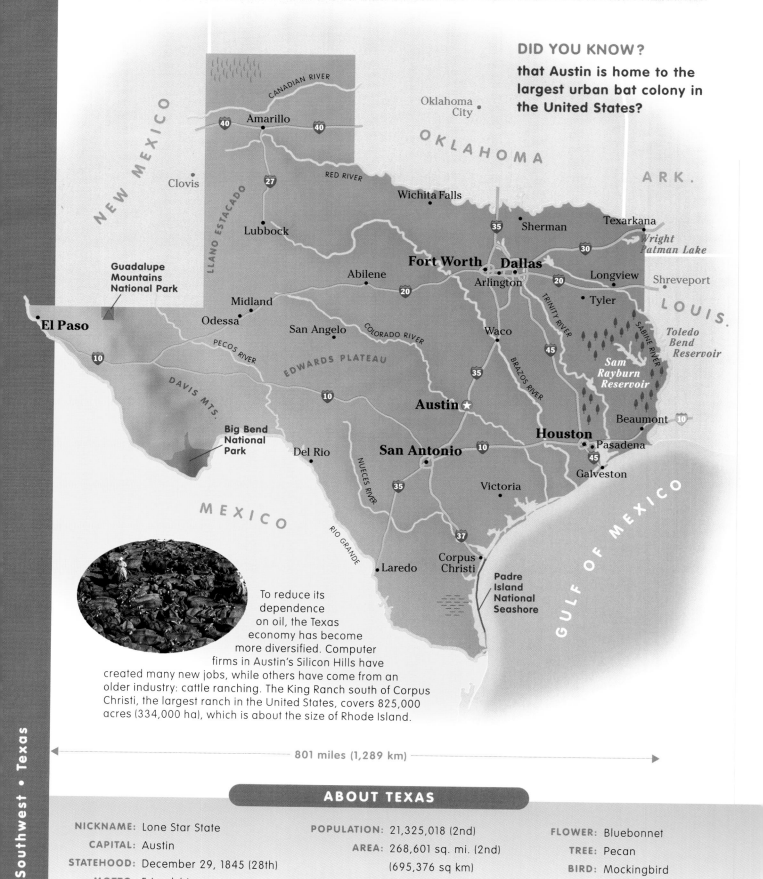

Interstate Highways State Capital National Parks and Refuges National Forests Marshes Grasslands Highest Point

0 miles 100
0 kilometers 161

DID YOU KNOW?

that Austin is home to the largest urban bat colony in the United States?

CANADIAN RIVER
Amarillo
40 40
Oklahoma City
OKLAHOMA
Clovis
RED RIVER
ARK.
27
Wichita Falls
Sherman
Texarkana
Lubbock
35
Wright Patman Lake
LLANO ESTACADO
30
Guadalupe Mountains National Park
Fort Worth Dallas
Longview
Shreveport
Abilene
Arlington
20
Tyler
Midland
20
LOUIS.
El Paso
Odessa
San Angelo
COLORADO RIVER
Waco
TRINITY RIVER
SABINE RIVER
10
PECOS RIVER
45
Sam Rayburn Reservoir
Toledo Bend Reservoir
DAVIS MTS.
EDWARDS PLATEAU
35
Big Bend National Park
Del Rio
10
Austin ★
BRAZOS RIVER
Beaumont
10
San Antonio
10
Houston
Pasadena
NUECES RIVER
45
Galveston
MEXICO
35
Victoria
RIO GRANDE
37
Laredo
Corpus Christi
Padre Island National Seashore
GULF OF MEXICO

NEW MEXICO

To reduce its dependence on oil, the Texas economy has become more diversified. Computer firms in Austin's Silicon Hills have created many new jobs, while others have come from an older industry: cattle ranching. The King Ranch south of Corpus Christi, the largest ranch in the United States, covers 825,000 acres (334,000 ha), which is about the size of Rhode Island.

801 miles (1,289 km)

ABOUT TEXAS

NICKNAME: Lone Star State
CAPITAL: Austin
STATEHOOD: December 29, 1845 (28th)
MOTTO: Friendship.

POPULATION: 21,325,018 (2nd)
AREA: 268,601 sq. mi. (2nd) (695,376 sq km)
HIGHEST POINT: 8,749 ft. (Guadalupe Peak)
LOWEST POINT: Sea level (Gulf of Mexico)

FLOWER: Bluebonnet
TREE: Pecan
BIRD: Mockingbird
FISH: Guadalupe bass

Texas

When Texas joined the Union in 1845, Congress gave it the right to divide itself into five states of more manageable size. Instead, Texas has remained huge—the second largest state, the second most populous, and among the wealthiest. Over the years, Texans have used their valuable natural resources, particularly oil, to fund the growth of profitable manufacturing industries, such as chemical production.

Houston, the center of the U.S. petroleum industry and one of the nation's busiest ports, sits on the Gulf Coastal Plain, which covers the state's eastern third. This highly industrialized and densely populated region includes Texas's best farmland and its most productive oil fields.

A line drawn from Fort Worth to San Antonio would separate the moist coastal plain from the dry, treeless hill country, where cattle ranching still dominates. Ranching is also the dominant industry on the High Plains of the Panhandle—where, it's said, the cowboy spirit endures. Farther south, in the Rio Grande Valley, an eleven-month growing season allows farmers to raise winter vegetables and some citrus fruit.

The Rio Grande Valley is also known for its high concentration of Mexican Americans. Hispanics account for nearly a third of Texas's population, making them an important political force in cities such as El Paso and San Antonio. In fact, census projections suggest that Texas will one day have a Hispanic majority.

Austin calls itself the Live Music Capital of the World because of the many nightclubs lining downtown Sixth Street. The diverse styles heard there include blues, country, jazz, swing, and Tejano.

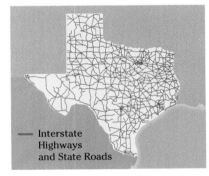

Interstate Highways and State Roads

Texas has more streets and highways than any other state. Its 294,833 total miles (474,386 km) are nearly twice that of second-place California. The state's annual roadway maintenance budget, which doesn't include money spent by towns or counties, is more than eight hundred million dollars, and its construction budget is nearly two billion dollars.

Texas boasts more than five thousand species of wildflowers. Although bluebonnet, pink evening primrose, and Indian paintbrush grow statewide, most varieties are confined to a particular region.

ARCTIC OCEAN

RUSSIA

BERING SEA

YUKON RIVER

Alaska
page 116

PACIFIC OCEAN

CANADA

Washington
page 124

COLUMBIA R.

SNAKE R.

Oregon
page 122

Hawaii
page 120

California
page 118

MEXICO

The Coast Ranges of California, Oregon, and Washington form a line along which the Pacific and North American plates (part of the earth's crust) crunch past one another. Earthquakes, with which most Californians are familiar, are one symptom of this stress. Another is volcanic activity, such as the eruption of Mount St. Helens in 1980. The Aleutian Islands of Alaska also sit on this Ring of Fire, the name given to the edge of the Pacific Plate along which most of the earth's active volcanoes are located.

Pacific

State Capital National Parks and Refuges Tundra Highest Point

| 0 | miles | 300 |
| 0 | km | 483 |

The Trans-Alaska Pipeline carries oil from Prudhoe Bay, where the coast is frozen eight months a year, to the ice-free port of Valdez eight hundred miles (1,300 km) away. Terrain permitting, the four-foot-wide (one-meter-wide) pipeline is buried. However, across the permanently frozen Arctic tundra, it's typically raised on supports that allow migrating caribou to pass underneath.

ARCTIC OCEAN

Barrow
• Prudhoe Bay

Chukchi Sea
NORTH SLOPE
COLVILLE RIVER
BROOKS RANGE
NOATAK RIVER

RUSSIA

⑦
⑧
Kotzebue

Bering Strait

PORCUPINE R.
YUKON RIVER

KOYUKUK R.

CANADA

Nome

YUKON RIVER
KUSKOKWIM MTS.
KUSKOKWIM RIVER
ALASKA RANGE

College • • Fairbanks
TANANA RIVER

BERING SEA

⑥
⑤
Bethel
Anchorage
• Kenai
Valdez •
• Cordova
WRANGELL MTS.
② Whitehorse

③
Prince William Sound

DID YOU KNOW?
that because the Matanuska Valley north of Anchorage gets twenty hours of sunlight during summer, cabbages there grow to nearly one hundred pounds (45 kg)?

④
• Skagway
① ★
Juneau
Sitka •
Alexander Archipelago
• Ketchikan

ALEUTIAN RANGE
• Kodiak
Kodiak Island
Gulf of Alaska

Cold Bay •

Unalaska •

Aleutian Islands

PACIFIC OCEAN

NATIONAL PARKS
① Glacier Bay
② Wrangell–St. Elias
③ Kenai Fjords
④ Katmai
⑤ Lake Clark
⑥ Denali
⑦ Gates of the Arctic
⑧ Kobuk Valley

2,400 miles (3,862 km)

ABOUT ALASKA

NICKNAME: Last Frontier
CAPITAL: Juneau
STATEHOOD: January 3, 1959 (49th)
MOTTO: North to the future.

POPULATION: 619,500 (48th)
AREA: 656,424 sq. mi. (1st)
(1,699,404 sq km)
HIGHEST POINT: 20,320 ft. (Mount McKinley)
LOWEST POINT: Sea level (Pacific Ocean)

FLOWER: Forget-me-not
TREE: Sitka spruce
BIRD: Willow ptarmigan
FISH: King salmon

Alaska

Alaska can be a hard place to live because of the cold climate and rough terrain. In January, for example, the temperature in Fairbanks rarely rises above 0°F (-18°C), and even during the summer months, mountain ranges and ice fields make ground-level travel difficult, as do the great distances involved.

Alaskans have made up for this isolation by using satellite telephones and the Internet to connect to the outside world. Among the most ardent users of these new technologies are the native people who make up 16 percent of the population. Even so, many Aleuts and Inuit still live off the land, hunting and fishing as their ancestors did.

The dominant physical feature of the Alaskan Panhandle is the Inside Passage, a sheltered waterway stretching from Skagway to Seattle, Washington. Through its channels runs the Alaska Marine Highway, a state-operated ferry system that services towns with little or no road access. Far more remote are the fogbound Aleutian Islands, jutting eleven hundred miles (1,800 km) into the North Pacific.

Inland, north of the Alaska Range, sits the Yukon Plateau, beyond which few Alaskans live. From the crest of the little-explored Brooks Range, the land slopes down to the Arctic Coastal Plain, where immense oil fields were discovered in 1968. Currently, oil revenues fund about 85 percent of the state budget, but Alaskans have also had to live with oil's environmental consequences, such as the 1989 *Exxon Valdez* spill that polluted Prince William Sound.

In rugged Alaska, the family "car" is often a small airplane. One out of every fifty-eight Alaskans has a license to fly, which is six times the national average. Even where there are roads, snowmobiles often take the place of cars in winter.

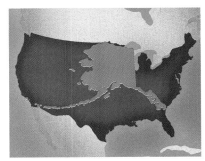

Alaska, the largest state, accounts for one sixth of the nation's total area. If you superimposed a map of Alaska on a map of the continental United States, Alaska would stretch all the way from Savannah, Georgia, to Los Angeles and reach as far north as the Canadian border.

The towering peaks of the Alaska Range dominate the southern half of the state. These include Mount McKinley, the highest point in North America. Of the twenty tallest U.S. mountains, seventeen are in Alaska.

Interstate Highways

State Capital

Native American Reservations

National Forests

National Parks and Refuges

Highest Point

miles 0 — 100
kilometers 0 — 161

OREGON

Redwood National Park

KLAMATH RIVER

KLAMATH MTS.

CASCADE MTS.

Goose Lake

Eureka

EEL RIVER

Redding

Lassen Volcanic National Park

Shasta Lake

COAST RANGES

Chico

SACRAMENTO R.

Clear Lake

SIERRA NEVADA

Reno

In California's fertile Central Valley, farmers grow more than 350 varieties of fruits and vegetables. When processed, these crops make up about 40 percent of the nation's canned and frozen produce. Supermarkets can sell California produce cheaply because much of it is picked by migrant workers who work under difficult conditions for little pay.

NEVADA

Santa Rosa

Sacramento

Lake Tahoe

Yosemite National Park

Mono Lake

MAJOR NATIVE AMERICAN RESERVATIONS

① Hoopa Valley
② Round Valley
③ Tule River
④ Aqua Caliente

Berkeley
San Francisco
Oakland
Stockton
Modesto
Merced

Sunnyvale
San Jose
Santa Cruz
Salinas
Monterey

SAN JOAQUIN R.

COAST RANGES

SALINAS RIVER

Fresno

Kings Canyon National Park

Death Valley National Park

Sequoia National Park

Las Vegas

San Luis Obispo

Bakersfield

Barstow

MOJAVE DESERT

ARIZONA

COLORADO RIVER

Santa Barbara

Pasadena
San Bernardino

Joshua Tree National Park

DID YOU KNOW?

that the highest (Mount Whitney) and the lowest (Death Valley) points in the continental United States are only sixty miles (97 km) apart?

PACIFIC OCEAN

Los Angeles
Anaheim
Riverside
Santa Ana

Long Beach

Channel Islands National Park

Channel Islands

San Diego
Chula Vista

Escondido

Salton Sea

Tijuana

MEXICO

350 miles (563 km)

ABOUT CALIFORNIA

NICKNAME: Golden State

CAPITAL: Sacramento

STATEHOOD: September 9, 1850 (31st)

MOTTO: Eureka!

POPULATION: 33,145,121 (1st)

AREA: 163,707 sq. mi. (3rd)
(423,818 sq km)

HIGHEST POINT: 14,494 ft. (Mount Whitney)

LOWEST POINT: -282 ft. (Death Valley)

FLOWER: Golden poppy

TREE: California redwood

BIRD: California valley quail

FISH: California golden trout

California

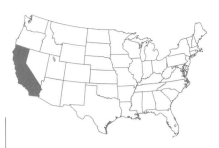

A century ago, immigrants from all over the world flocked to New York City to earn their fortunes. Since World War II, however, even New Yorkers have gone to California to make their dreams come true—and not just out-of-work actors. Today, it's impossible to overstate California's economic, political, and cultural importance. The state ranks first in both manufactured goods and farm income, and without California's votes it's difficult to win a presidential election. Cultural trends, too, now move from west to east: Two recent examples are organic foods and eastern religion (no doubt influenced by the many Asian Americans living in California). Overall, nearly one in eight Americans is a Californian, including half of all Mexican Americans and two fifths of all Asian Americans, many of whom are recent immigrants.

Although southern California is famous for its beaches, most of it sits on the Mojave Desert. As a result, the region has 50 percent of the state's population but only 2 percent of its water. That's why a complex system of dams and aqueducts has been built to divert water from elsewhere, principally the Colorado River.

North of the fertile Central Valley, which runs between the Coast Ranges and the Sierra Nevada, the Klamath and Cascade mountains rise above dense stands of timber. Except in the desert south, California has two seasons: a dry one from spring to fall and a rainy one the rest of the year.

Alice Waters, the founder of Berkeley's Chez Panisse restaurant, began a trend in cooking that has since come to be known as California cuisine. Her cooking emphasizes the freshest ingredients, usually grown organically on small local farms, and borrows freely from California's many immigrant cuisines, especially Asian and Mexican.

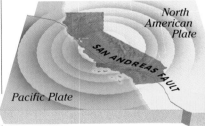

In earthquake-prone California, two of the plates that make up the earth's crust come together. The line along which they meet is called the San Andreas Fault. As the Pacific Plate creeps northwestward, it pushes against the North American Plate, causing pressure to build. From time to time, this pressure is released as an earthquake.

California's largest cities are all located at gaps in the Coast Ranges. Elsewhere, these mountains rise so abruptly from the Pacific that towns have no room to grow. There's barely enough room for State Route 1, which is often closed by mud slides.

LEGEND

⭐ State Capital

■ National Parks and Refuges

▲ Highest Point

| 0 | miles | 100 |
| 0 | kilometers | 161 |

DID YOU KNOW?

that despite the tropical climate, snow falls on Hawaii's tallest mountains?

Kauai

Kapaa
Kekaha • Lihue
Puuwai

Niihau

Oahu

Pearl City • Kaneohe
Waipahu • • Kailua
⭐ **Honolulu**
Pearl Harbor

Molokai
Kaunakakai

Maui
Lanai City • Wailuku
• Kahului
Kihei •
Haleakala National Park

Lanai

Kahoolawe

P A C I F I C   O C E A N

Hawaii
Waimea •
Kailua-Kona •
WAILUKU R.
Captain Cook •
Hilo •
▲

Hawaii Volcanoes National Park

Ka Lae •

Hawaii leads the nation in raising bananas, papayas, guavas, macadamia nuts, and coffee, as well as pineapples, the state's most famous crop. Each year, the pineapple harvest brings in about one hundred million dollars.

353 miles (568 km)

ABOUT HAWAII

NICKNAME: Aloha State

CAPITAL: Honolulu

STATEHOOD: August 21, 1959 (50th)

MOTTO: The life of the land is perpetuated in righteousness.

POPULATION: 1,185,497 (42nd)

AREA: 10,932 sq. mi. (43rd) (28,302 sq km)

HIGHEST POINT: 13,796 ft. (Mauna Kea)

LOWEST POINT: Sea level (Pacific Ocean)

FLOWER: Yellow hibiscus

TREE: Kukui (candlenut)

BIRD: Nene (Hawaiian goose)

Hawaii

The familiar Hawaiian islands are, in fact, the eastern end of a sixteen-hundred-mile (twenty-six-hundred-kilometer) chain stretching from the Big Island of Hawaii northwest to tiny Kure Atoll. Nearly all Hawaiians live on the eight major islands, which are the cone-shaped tops of gigantic ocean volcanoes. Of these people, 21 percent are descendants of the Polynesians who originally settled Hawaii. The rest are 33 percent white, 20 percent Japanese, 10 percent Filipino, 3 percent Chinese, and 3 percent black, giving Hawaii the most diverse ethnic mix of any state.

Even so, Hawaii's population is dwarfed each year by the seven million tourists who bring with them ten billion dollars, by far the state's largest source of income. The next largest revenue producer is the federal government. Military bases such as Pearl Harbor house so many soldiers and sailors that military personnel and their families make up nearly one tenth of the state's population.

The most crowded island is Oahu, where about three in four Hawaiians live. The largest island is agricultural Hawaii. Kauai's lush valleys, Maui's wide beaches, and Lanai's seclusion are particularly popular with tourists, while Molokai and Niihau have especially high concentrations of native Hawaiians. On the tiny, privately owned island of Niihau, several hundred pure-blood Hawaiians raise livestock, speak their traditional language, and otherwise struggle to keep native traditions alive. Public access to Niihau is strictly limited, and no one at all is allowed on Kahoolawe, which until recently was a bombing range.

"Shaka, Brah"

Among young people in Hawaii, the "shaka" sign is the universal greeting. Given with the thumb pointing up and the pinkie pointing out, it means both "hello" and "peace"—and, more generally— "good vibes." It's often accompanied by the phrase "Shaka, Brah." (*Brah* is pidgin English for "brother.")

Mauna Kea

Mount Everest

33,476 ft (10,203 m)

29,035 ft (8,850 m)

The state's highest point, Mauna Kea on the Big Island of Hawaii, rises 13,796 feet (4,205 m) above sea level. It also extends nearly 20,000 feet (6,000 m) down to the bottom of the Hawaiian Trough. If you count this submerged base, Mauna Kea becomes the tallest mountain in the world, topping even Mount Everest.

The white sand that covers most Hawaiian beaches is made of tiny shell and coral fragments pulverized by the pounding surf. Some beaches, however, have black sand made of crushed obsidian, which is also called volcanic glass.

LEGEND

20	⬙	▢	🌲	◼	▲	0	miles 100
Interstate Highways	State Capital	Native American Reservations	National Forests	National Parks and Refuges	Highest Point	0	kilometers 161

Although the timber industry no longer dominates the state economy, it remains important to the way that Oregonians view themselves. Each July, for example, the Albany Timber Carnival sponsors popular competitions in log chopping, sawing, ax throwing, and birling (log rolling in water).

WASHINGTON

Kennewick

Astoria

Portland

Vancouver

The Dalles

COLUMBIA RIVER

Pendleton

Umatilla Reservation

Beaverton

Gresham

DESCHUTES R.

McMinnville

WILLAMETTE R.

La Grande

BLUE MOUNTAINS

★ **Salem**

Warm Springs Reservation

JOHN DAY R.

Baker City

Albany

Corvallis

Canyon City

SNAKE RIVER

IDAHO

PACIFIC OCEAN

Eugene

Springfield

Bend

Ontario

HARNEY BASIN

Boise

Coos Bay

UMPQUA RIVER

Roseburg

Crater Lake National Park

Harney Lake

Malheur Lake

COAST RANGES

ROGUE RIVER

Summer Lake

STEENS MOUNTAINS

ALVORD DESERT

Upper Klamath Lake

Lake Abert

Grants Pass

Medford

Ashland

Klamath Falls

Altamont

Goose Lake

KLAMATH RIVER

CALIFORNIA

NEVADA

CASCADE RANGE

OWYHEE RIVER

DID YOU KNOW?

that Oregon, a national leader in ecological legislation, passed the nation's first bottle-return law in 1971?

395 miles (636 km)

ABOUT OREGON

NICKNAME: Beaver State

CAPITAL: Salem

STATEHOOD: February 14, 1859 (33rd)

MOTTO: She flies with her own wings.

POPULATION: 3,316,154 (28th)

AREA: 98,386 sq. mi. (9th) (254,710 sq km)

HIGHEST POINT: 11,239 ft. (Mount Hood)

LOWEST POINT: Sea level (Pacific Ocean)

FLOWER: Oregon grape

TREE: Douglas fir

BIRD: Western meadowlark

FISH: Chinook salmon

Oregon

No one doubts that Oregonians love the outdoors. Excluding the state's passion for wrestling, bicycling and long-distance running are its most high-profile sports. Yet Oregon is also the nation's leading timber state, and until recently most Oregonians worked for timber-related companies. During the 1990s, though, they had to make hard choices between their jobs and the environment.

Some choices were made for them. To protect the habitat of the endangered northern spotted owl, the federal government severely restricted logging in public forests, which contain about half of Oregon's timber. In response, the state reduced its dependence on forestry by promoting high-tech industries like those in neighboring Washington and California.

Recent immigrants to Oregon say that they value the state's high quality of life, particularly its clean air and water, outdoor lifestyle, and many open spaces. In fact, outside the Willamette River Valley, Oregon is quite sparsely settled. The rainy, foggy, populated Oregon that most people picture in their minds exists only west of the Cascades. The rest of the state sits mostly on the dry, barren Columbia Plateau. Geologists call the land south of the Blue Mountains the High Lava Plains because it was once covered with lava from the volcano that erupted to form Crater Lake. To most people, though, this Utah-like landscape is simply the Oregon Desert.

Bicycle-friendly Portland has recently become even more so. In 1994, a community-based environmental group interested in reducing auto pollution began leaving free bicycles around the city for anyone to use. Riders are merely asked to return the bikes, painted a distinctive yellow, to a main street after each trip.

Nearly eight thousand years ago, a volcano erupted in southern Oregon. The explosion blew off the mountain's peak, leaving behind a crater that has since filled with rainwater and snowmelt. Intensely blue Crater Lake is, at 1,932 feet (589 m), the deepest lake in the United States and the seventh deepest in the world.

Most Oregonians live in the fertile Willamette River Valley, running south from the Columbia River between the Coast Range and the Cascades. Many farms there grow flowering bulbs and plants such as tulips and the irises pictured at left.

123

LEGEND

🛣 Interstate Highways ✪ State Capital ⬜ Native American Reservations 🌲 National Forests ⬛ National Parks and Refuges 🔺 Highest Point

| 0 | miles | 100 |
| 0 | kilometers | 161 |

DID YOU KNOW?

that the San Juan Islands in Puget Sound increase from 428 to 743 islands between high and low tides?

CANADA

Vancouver
Point Roberts
North Cascades National Park
Bellingham
San Juan Islands
Strait of San Juan de Fuca
Puget Sound
SKAGIT RIVER
Colville Reservation
KETTLE RIVER RANGE
COLUMBIA RIVER
Port Angeles
Everett
CASCADE RANGE
Lake Chelan
WENATCHEE MTS.
Spokane Reservation
Olympic National Park
OLYMPIC MTS.
Seattle
Bellevue
Banks Lake
Grand Coulee
SPOKANE RIVER
Spokane
Federal Way
Wenatchee
Quinault Reservation
COAST RANGES
Tacoma
90
Ephrata
Moses Lake
90
IDAHO
Aberdeen
Olympia
Ellensburg
Potholes Reservoir
Centralia
Mount Rainier National Park
Yakima
COLUMBIA RIVER
SNAKE RIVER
Longview
Kelso
Richland
Kennewick
Walla Walla
Mt. St. Helens National Volcanic Monument
Vancouver
YAKIMA RIVER
82
Yakima Reservation
Portland
OREGON
PACIFIC OCEAN

Dams on the Snake and Columbia rivers produce about one third of all U.S. hydroelectric power. The most impressive is the Grand Coulee Dam, the nation's largest concrete structure. Many Washington businesses depend on its cheap renewable energy, such as the Reynolds Metals aluminum-smelting plant in Longview.

← 360 miles (579 km) →

ABOUT WASHINGTON

NICKNAME: Evergreen State
CAPITAL: Olympia
STATEHOOD: November 11, 1889 (42nd)
MOTTO: By and by.

POPULATION: 5,756,361 (15th)
AREA: 71,302 sq. mi. (18th) (184,592 sq km)
HIGHEST POINT: 14,410 ft. (Mount Rainier)
LOWEST POINT: Sea level (Pacific Ocean)

FLOWER: Coast rhododendron
TREE: Western hemlock
BIRD: Willow goldfinch
FISH: Steelhead trout

Washington

Besides the rain, what's not to like about Washington? From the snowcapped mountains to the islands of Puget Sound, the scenery is spectacular, and the state's economy is equally breathtaking. Perhaps that's why Seattle has become one of the nation's most desirable and fastest-growing cities.

About two thirds of the state's population lives on the shores of Puget Sound, where shipbuilding used to be the leading industry. Now it's computers. Boasting more than two thousand software companies, notably Microsoft, the Puget Sound basin has come to rival California's Silicon Valley as the nation's leading high-tech, high-wage center.

Elsewhere in western Washington, forestry companies harvest the abundant timber growing on the western slopes of the Olympic and Cascade mountains. That's where most of the rain falls, as much as two hundred inches (500 cm) per year. All that moisture nourishes a unique temperate rain forest thickly carpeted with ferns and mosses.

Yet just a few miles over the Cascades in eastern Washington, the Columbia Plateau is so dry that dams are needed to irrigate the fields. With enough water, though, the rich volcanic soil of the Columbia Plateau is well suited to agriculture. Among the most valuable crops grown there are apples, cherries, asparagus, raspberries, and wine grapes. The warm days, cool nights, and sandy soil of the Columbia River basin resemble the vineyard conditions in France, making for excellent grape growing.

As well as skiing, sailing, and mountain climbing, Washingtonians are particularly fond of wildlife watching. The ferry that carries commuters from the San Juan Islands to Seattle also provides the occasional opportunity to view the orcas, minke whales, and seals that live in Puget Sound.

Why is western Washington so wet and eastern Washington so dry? Because the height of the Cascades forces clouds to drop their moisture before passing over. That's why the Olympic Peninsula receives 125 inches (318 cm) of precipitation per year and Richland on the Columbia River only 7 inches (18 cm).

Most of the high peaks in the Cascades are dormant volcanoes, yet every so often one becomes active. On May 18, 1980, long-dormant Mount St. Helens erupted, blanketing most of the Northwest with volcanic ash.

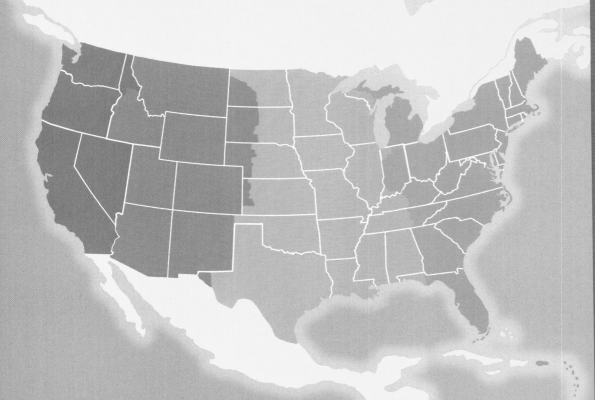

4 A.M.   5 A.M.   6 A.M.   7 A.M.

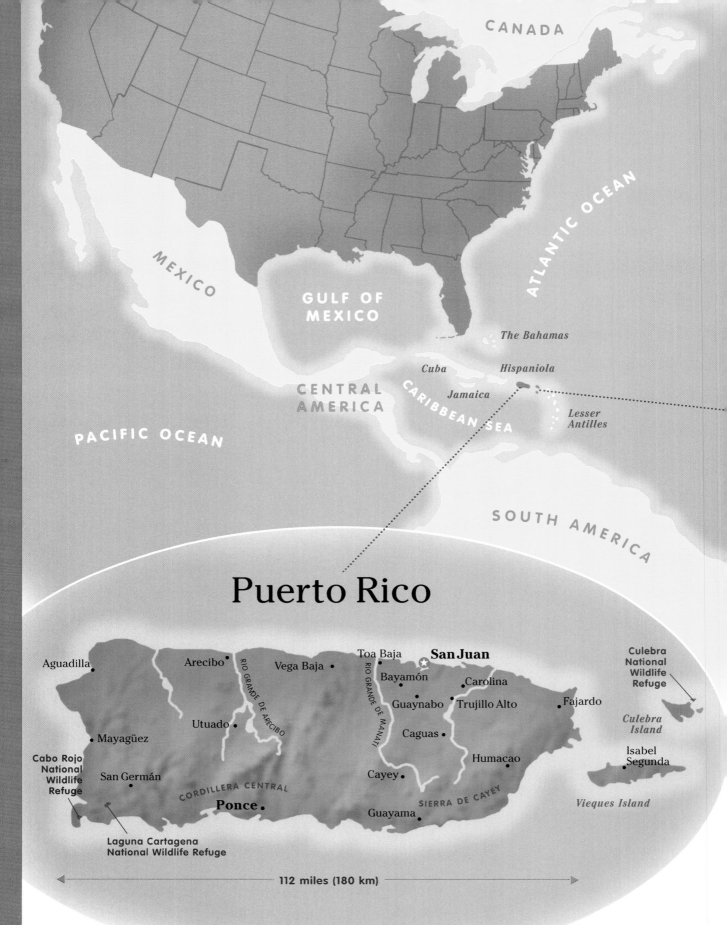

CANADA

ATLANTIC OCEAN

MEXICO

GULF OF
MEXICO

The Bahamas

Cuba

Hispaniola

CENTRAL
AMERICA

Jamaica

CARIBBEAN SEA

*Lesser
Antilles*

PACIFIC OCEAN

SOUTH AMERICA

Puerto Rico

Aguadilla

Arecibo

Vega Baja

Toa Baja

San Juan

Culebra
National
Wildlife
Refuge

RIO GRANDE DE ARECIBO

Bayamón

Carolina

*Culebra
Island*

Utuado

Guaynabo

Trujillo Alto

Fajardo

RIO GRANDE DE MANATI

Mayagüez

Caguas

Cabo Rojo
National
Wildlife
Refuge

San Germán

Humacao

Isabel
Segunda

CORDILLERA CENTRAL

Cayey

Ponce

SIERRA DE CAYEY

Vieques Island

Laguna Cartagena
National Wildlife
Refuge

Guayama

112 miles (180 km)

Atlantic Possessions

St. Thomas

★ **Charlotte Amalie**

St. John

Virgin Islands National Park

U.S. Virgin Islands

|←—————— 35 miles (56 km) ——————→|

Green Cay National Wildlife Refuge

Buck Island Reef National Monument

St. Croix

Christiansted •

Sandy Point National Wildlife Refuge

Frederiksted •

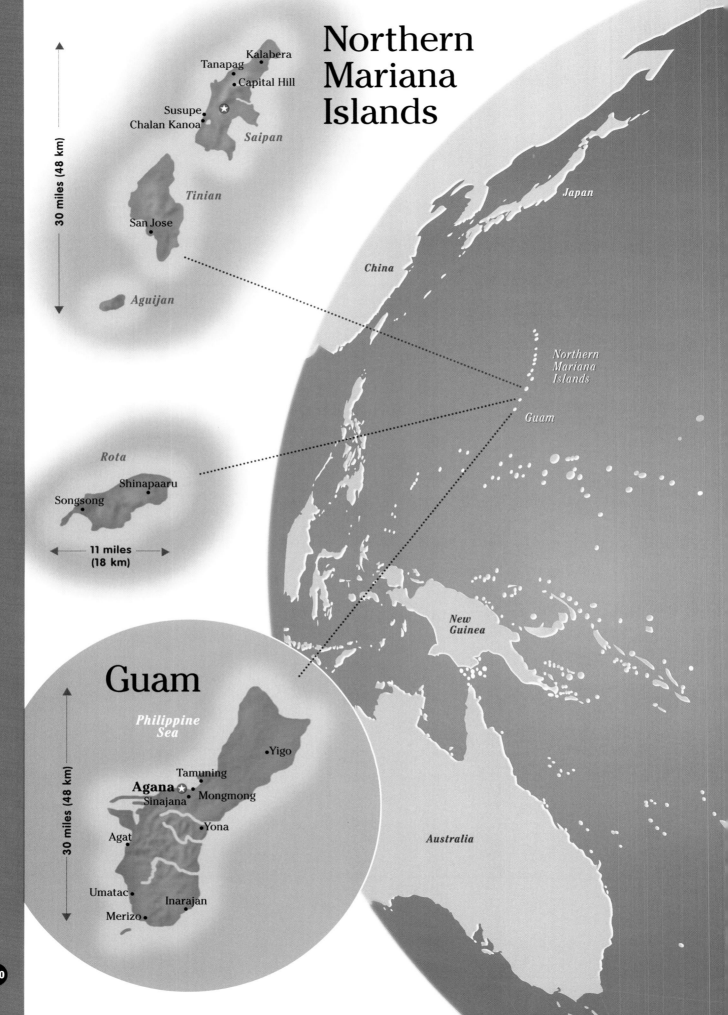

Northern Mariana Islands

Kalabera

Tanapag

Capital Hill

Susupe

Chalan Kanoa

Saipan

30 miles (48 km)

Tinian

San Jose

Aguijan

Rota

Shinapaaru

Songsong

11 miles
(18 km)

Guam

*Philippine
Sea*

•Yigo

Tamuning

Agana

Sinajana   Mongmong

•Yona

Agat

Umatac   •Inarajan

Merizo•

30 miles (48 km)

Japan

China

*Northern
Mariana
Islands*

Guam

*New
Guinea*

Australia

Pacific Possessions

Aleutian Islands

PACIFIC OCEAN

Hawaii

American Samoa

National Park of American Samoa

Tutuila

• Tula

★ **Pago Pago** • Fagatogo

Aunuu

• Nuuuli

Leone •

• Iliili

**20 miles
(32 km)**

Olosega

Ofu

Tau

Tau • • Maia

Manua Islands

National Park of American Samoa

**18 miles
(29 km)**

American Samoa

Western Samoa

Fiji

Tonga

U.S. Population Density

CANADA

PACIFIC OCEAN

MEXICO

GULF OF MEXICO

ATLANTIC OCEAN

POPULATION DENSITY
(people per square mile)

fewer than 2

2 to 24

25 to 125

more than 125

Major U.S. River Systems

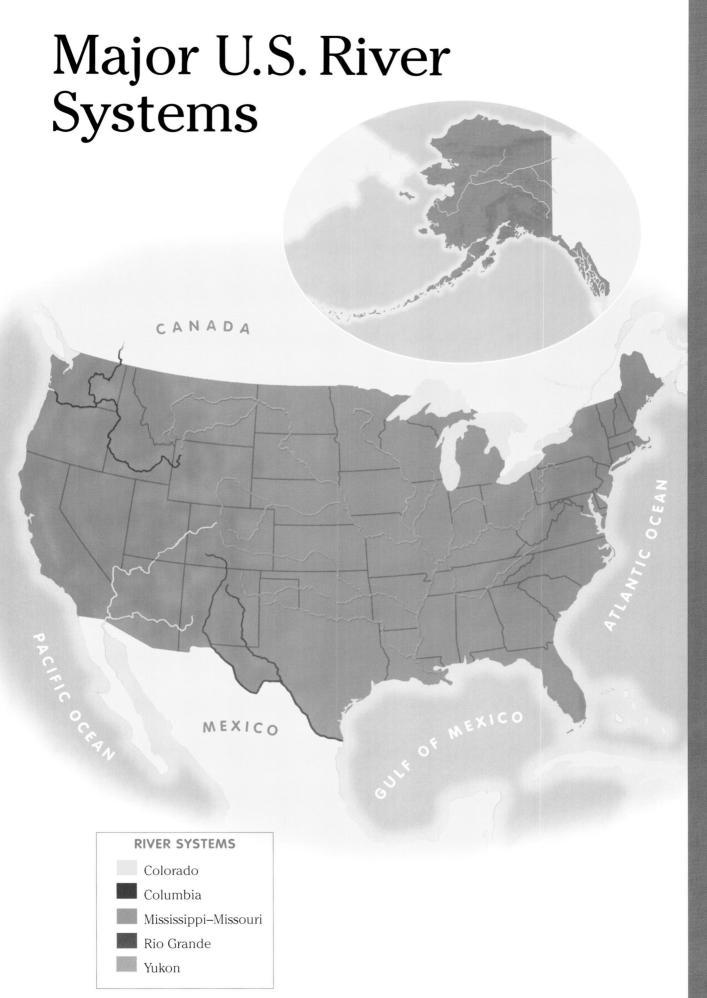

CANADA

ALASKA

PACIFIC OCEAN

MEXICO

GULF OF MEXICO

ATLANTIC OCEAN

RIVER SYSTEMS
- Colorado
- Columbia
- Mississippi–Missouri
- Rio Grande
- Yukon

U.S. Geographic Regions

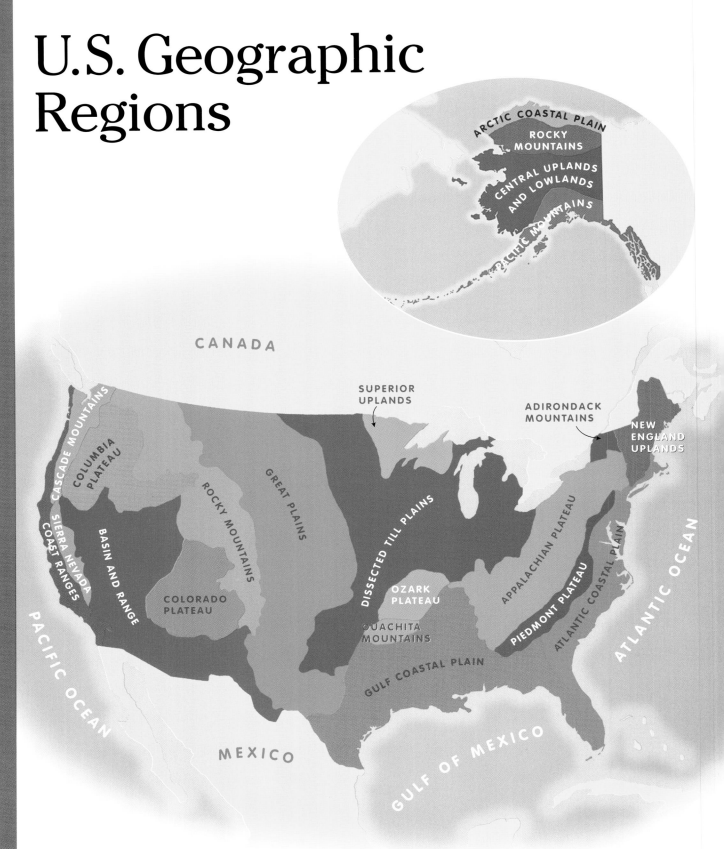

ARCTIC COASTAL PLAIN

ROCKY MOUNTAINS

CENTRAL UPLANDS AND LOWLANDS

PACIFIC MOUNTAINS

CANADA

SUPERIOR UPLANDS

ADIRONDACK MOUNTAINS

NEW ENGLAND UPLANDS

CASCADE MOUNTAINS

COLUMBIA PLATEAU

ROCKY MOUNTAINS

GREAT PLAINS

DISSECTED TILL PLAINS

APPALACHIAN PLATEAU

SIERRA NEVADA COAST RANGES

BASIN AND RANGE

COLORADO PLATEAU

OZARK PLATEAU

OUACHITA MOUNTAINS

PIEDMONT PLATEAU

ATLANTIC COASTAL PLAIN

ATLANTIC OCEAN

PACIFIC OCEAN

GULF COASTAL PLAIN

MEXICO

GULF OF MEXICO

U.S. Territorial Expansion

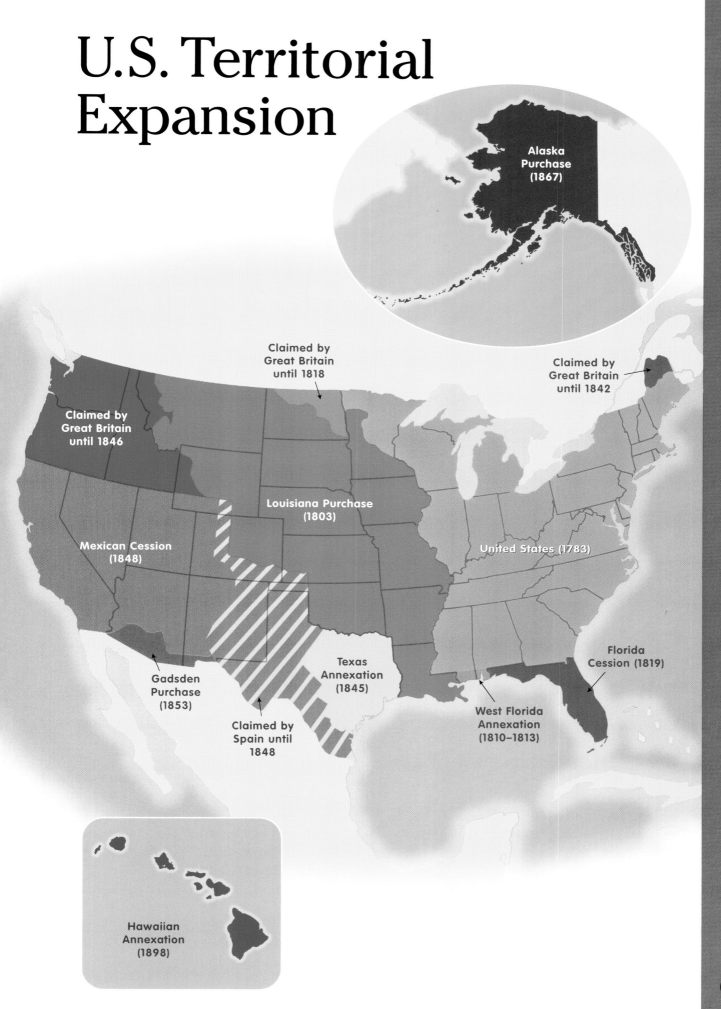

Alaska Purchase (1867)

Claimed by Great Britain until 1818

Claimed by Great Britain until 1842

Claimed by Great Britain until 1846

Louisiana Purchase (1803)

United States (1783)

Mexican Cession (1848)

Gadsden Purchase (1853)

Claimed by Spain until 1848

Texas Annexation (1845)

West Florida Annexation (1810–1813)

Florida Cession (1819)

Hawaiian Annexation (1898)

Glossary

aquifer an underground layer of rock, sand, or gravel that holds water

arable suitable for growing crops

arid excessively dry; also, receiving too little rainfall to support agriculture

atoll a coral island consisting of a reef encircling a lagoon

bald a treeless hilltop

basin a depression in the earth's surface; also, the area drained by a river and its tributaries

bayou a slow-moving creek

bedrock solid rock underlying a surface layer of soil

bluff a high steep bank or cliff

bog an area of wet, spongy ground

bottomland a low-lying region along a waterway

butte an isolated hill or mountain with steep sides (smaller than a mesa)

canal an artificial waterway constructed to aid navigation

canyon a deep narrow valley with steep sides, often with a stream or river flowing through it

channel a narrow passage of sea between two close landmasses

Continental Divide the principal watershed of North America, separating the Atlantic and Pacific ocean basins

continental United States the coterminous landmass of the United States, composed of forty-eight states (excluding Alaska and Hawaii)

crater the bowl-shaped depression atop a volcano

delta the land created by sediment deposits at the mouth of a river

divide a watershed, or dividing ridge between drainage areas

drift debris transported by a glacier

escarpment a cliff or steep slope between two level surfaces

estuary the area in which an ocean tide meets a river current

fall line the line along which a plateau drops abruptly, creating river rapids and waterfalls

fault a fracture in the earth's crust

floodplain level land occasionally submerged by floodwaters

foothills hilly region at the base of a mountain range

front the line defining the base of a mountain range

glaciation the process, or result, of being covered by a glacier

glacier a huge sheet of ice

gorge a narrow canyon

head of navigation the point on a river past which ships cannot travel

kettle lake a steep-sided lake formed by a glacier

levee a raised structure built to keep a river within its channel (and thereby prevent flooding)

loess soil composed of dirt deposited by the wind

mesa an isolated, flat-topped elevation of land (smaller than a plateau)

monadnock an isolated plug of granite that becomes a mountain after the surrounding land erodes away

oxbow lake a curved lake formed when a meandering river takes a more direct course, isolating a bend

peninsula a spit of land bounded on three sides by water

plateau a large, generally flat area rising above the surrounding land on at least one side

prairie mostly level or rolling land characterized by deep fertile soil, plentiful grass, and few trees

precipitation water deposited by clouds in the form of hail, mist, rain, sleet, or snow

rangeland land suitable for grazing livestock

sediment material deposited by water, wind, or glaciers

silt sediment deposited by moving water

subsoil the layer of weathered material underneath the topsoil

tableland broad, level, elevated land, as a plateau

terminal moraine rocky debris deposited at the front edge of a glacier

tidal river a river whose current is periodically affected (or reversed) by the force of ocean tides

tidewater low-lying coastal land characterized by numerous tidal rivers

till glacial drift containing a mixture of clay, sand, gravel, and boulders

topography the physical features of a region of land

topsoil the organic layer of soil closest to the surface into which plants sink their roots

tributary a river or stream that flows into a larger watercourse

tundra a level or rolling treeless plain with a permanently frozen subsoil

watershed a region, bounded by divides, draining into a particular body of water

Index

Photo Credits

Greater Hartford Tourism District/Paul Conee: 10; Robert Perron: 11(l); Mohegan Sun: 11(r); Northern Maine Development Commission: 12; Acadia National Park: 13(l); Kindra Clineff: 13(r), 14, 15(l); Genetics Institute/Susan Lapides: 15(r); Tom Pantages: 16; New Hampshire Office of Travel and Tourism Development: 17(l); Rhode Island Tourism Division: 18, 19(l); Vermont Department of Tourism and Marketing: 20, 21(l); Delaware Tourism Office: 25(l); Winterthur Museum: 25(r); Baltimore Orioles/Jerry Wachter: 26; Maryland Film Office: 27(r); Port Authority of New York and New Jersey: 28; New Jersey Agricultural Society: 29(l); New Jersey Commerce & Economic Growth Commission/Scott Barrow: 23, 29(r); New York Stock Exchange: 30; New York State Department of Economic Development: 31(both); Hershey Community Archives: 32; Commonwealth Media Services: 33(l); Pennsylvania Game Commission: 33(r); Julia Rubel: 34; Alabama Bureau of Tourism & Travel: 38, 39(r); Alabama Farmers Federation: 37, 39(l); National Chicken Council/Richard Lobb: 40; Arkansas Department of Parks & Tourism/A. C. Haralson: 41(both); Everglades National Park 43(l); Greater Miami Convention & Visitors Bureau/Carl Purcell: 43(r); Georgia Department of Industry, Trade & Tourism: 44; Carpet and Rug Institute: 45(r); Kentucky Department of Surface Mining: 46; Kentucky Department of Travel: 47(both); Louisiana Office of Tourism: 49(r); Catfish Farmers of America: 50; Robert Perron: 51(l); Oxford Tourism Council/Ken Murphy: 51(r); North Carolina Division of Tourism, Film & Sports Development: 52; Dare County Tourist Bureau: 53(l); Cherokee Tribal Travel & Promotion Office: 53(r); CMI Industries: 54; Myrtle Beach Area Chamber of Commerce: 55(l); Oak Ridge National Laboratory: 56(both); Great Smoky Mountains National Park: 57(l); Tennessee Tourist Development: 57(r); Newport News Shipbuilding: 58; Virginia Tourism Corporation: 59(l); Colonial Williamsburg Foundation: 59(r); West Virginia Division of Tourism/Gerald S. Ratliff: 60; Monongahela National Forest: 61(l); West Virginia Public Radio: 61(r); Highway Images/Bette S. Garber: 64; City of Chicago/Peter J. Schulz: 65(l); Indiana Geological Survey: 67(l); Indiana High School Athletic Association/Mark Wick: 67(r); Jolly Time Pop Corn: 68; Iowa Division of Tourism/Bob Coyle: 69(l); University of Iowa/Tom Jorgensen: 69(r); Ford Motor Company: 70; Travel Michigan: 71(l); Wisconsin Department of Tourism: 71(r); Cliffs Mining Services: 72; Minnesota Office of Tourism: 73(l); Minnesota Public Radio/Fredric Petters: 73(r); Fire Master Fire Engines: 74; Missouri Division of Tourism: 75(l); Truman Library: 75(r); Akron/Summit Convention & Visitors Bureau: 76; Ohio Division of Travel and Tourism: 77(both); Miller Brewing: 78; Wisconsin Department of Tourism: 79(l); EAA/Ken Lechtenberg: 79(r); Raytheon: 82; Kansas Wheat Commission: 83(l); *Emporia Gazette:* 83(r); National Cattlemen's Beef Association: 84; Stock Boston/Michael Collier: 85(l); University of Nebraska Athletic Department/ Joe Mixan: 85(r); North Dakota Wheat Commission/ Norma Anderson: 86; OBS Specialty Vehicles: 87(r); Citibank (South Dakota), N.A.: 88; South Dakota Tourism: 89(both); North American Aerospace Defense Command: 92; Colorado Travel & Tourism Authority: 93(l); Keystone Mountain/Ben Blankenburg: 93(r); Clear Springs Foods: 94; Nez Perce National Forest: 95(l); Peregrine Fund/ Russell Thorstrom: 95(r); Brodin Landing Nets: 96; Glacier National Park: 97(l); Travel Montana/M. Gurnett: 97(r); Thiokol Corporation: 98; Utah Travel Council: 99(both); Petroleum Association of Wyoming: 100; Wyoming Division of Tourism: 101(l); Cheyenne Frontier Days: 101(r); ASARCO: 104; Metropolitan Tucson Convention & Visitors Bureau/Gill Kenny: 105(both); Las Vegas News Bureau: 106; Mark Farmer: 107(r); Los Alamos National Laboratory/ Leroy Sanchez: 108; Taos County Chamber of Commerce/Susan Christie: 109(l); Indian Pueblo Cultural Center: 109(r); Oklahoma Tourism/Fred W. Marvel: 110; Samuel Roberts Noble Foundation: 111(l); King Ranch, Kingsville, Texas: 112; Wildseed Farms: 113(l); Austin Convention & Visitors Bureau: 113(r); Alyeska Pipeline: 116; National Park Service/Bob Richey: 117(l); Anchorage Convention & Visitors Bureau: 117(r); California Division of Tourism/Robert Holmes: 119(l); Chez Panisse/Franklin Avery: 119(r); Hawaii Visitors & Convention Bureau: 120, 121(l); Lewis Rosman: 121(r); Oregon Tourism Commission: 122, 123(l); David Falconer: 123(r); Bureau of Reclamation: 124; Mount St. Helens National Volcanic Monument: 125(l); Bellingham/Whatcom County Convention & Visitors Bureau: 125(r); Corbis: 9, 17(r), 19(r), 21(r), 24, 27(l), 35(both), 42, 45(l), 48, 49(l), 55(r), 63, 65(r) 66, 81, 87(l), 91, 103, 107(l), 111(r), 115, 118.